Australian Political Lives

Chronicling political careers and administrative histories

Australian Political Lives

Chronicling political careers and administrative histories

Tracey Arklay, John Nethercote
and John Wanna, editors

ANU
THE AUSTRALIAN NATIONAL UNIVERSITY

E PRESS

ANU

E PRESS

·: ···
· ·· ·
·

the Australia and New Zealand
School of Government

Published by ANU E Press
The Australian National University
Canberra ACT 0200, Australia
Email: anuepress@anu.edu.au
Web: http://epress.anu.edu.au

National Library of Australia
Cataloguing-in-Publication entry

Nethercote, J. R. (John Raymond).
Australian political lives : chronicling political careers
and administrative histories

Bibliography
Includes index
ISBN 1 920942 73 4 (pbk.)
ISBN 1 920942 74 2 (online)

1. Politicians - Australia - Biography - History and
criticism. 2. Campaign biography - Australia. I. Wanna,
John. II. Arklay, Tracy. III. Title.

808.066320092

Cover design by John Butcher

Funding for this monograph series has been provided by the Australia and New
Zealand School of Government Research Program.

John Wanna, *Series Editor*

Professor John Wanna is the Sir John Bunting Chair of Public Administration at the Research School of Social Sciences at The Australian National University. He is the director of research for the Australian and New Zealand School of Government (ANZSOG). He is also a joint appointment with the Department of Politics and Public Policy at Griffith University and a principal researcher with two research centres: the Governance and Public Policy Research Centre and the nationally-funded Key Centre in Ethics, Law, Justice and Governance at Griffith University. Professor Wanna has produced around 17 books including two national text books on policy and public management. He has produced a number of research-based studies on budgeting and financial management including: *Budgetary Management and Control* (1990); *Managing Public Expenditure* (2000), *From Accounting to Accountability* (2001) and, most recently, *Controlling Public Expenditure* (2003). He has just completed a study of state level leadership covering all the state and territory leaders — entitled *Yes Premier: Labor leadership in Australia's states and territories* — and has edited a book on Westminster Legacies in Asia and the Pacific — *Westminster Legacies: Democracy and responsible government in Asia and the Pacific*. He was a chief investigator in a major Australian Research Council funded study of the Future of Governance in Australia (1999-2001) involving Griffith and the ANU. His research interests include Australian and comparative politics, public expenditure and budgeting, and government-business relations. He also writes on Australian politics in newspapers such as *The Australian*, *Courier-Mail* and *Canberra Times* and has been a regular state political commentator on ABC radio and TV.

Table of Contents

List of Contributors

Tracey Arklay is a doctoral student at Griffith University, Queensland, and is writing a biography of Sir Arthur Fadden. She recently worked as a research assistant on the History of the Queensland Parliament 1957-89 project.

Neal Blewett, AC, was Professor of Political Theory, Flinders University, South Australia from 1974-77, member of the House of Representatives from 1977-94, minister in the Hawke-Keating governments from1983-93, and Australian High Commissioner in London from 1994-98. He is the author of *A Cabinet Diary* (1999).

Geoffrey Bolton, AO, Chancellor, Murdoch University, WA, has held chairs in history at Murdoch, London, Queensland and Edith Cowan universities. Author of biographies of Sir Richard Boyer (1967) and Sir Edmund Barton (2000), he is now writing a biography of Sir Paul Hasluck.

Judith Brett, Professor of Politics, Latrobe University, Victoria. She is the author of *Australian Liberals and the Moral Middle Class: From Alfred Deakin to John Howard* (2003) and *Robert Menzies' Forgotten People* (2002). Her edited book, *Political Lives*, was published in 1997.

Nicholas Brown is Senior Research Fellow at the *Australian Dictionary of Biography*, located in the Research School of Social Sciences at The Australian National University. He is the author of *Richard Downing: Economics, advocacy and social reform in Australia* (2001).

John Button was Labor Senator for Victoria from1974-93, Leader of the Government in the Senate from 1983-93 and Minister for Industry from 1983-93. He is the author of *As It Happened* (1998).

Lenore Coltheart taught political history in Australian universities for 25 years before retiring to Canberra in 1997. She prepared a revised edition of Jessie Street's autobiography, *Jessie Street: A revised autobiography* (2004) and is currently writing a biography of Jesse Street.

David Day is a Research Fellow in the School of Historical and European Studies at Latrobe University, Victoria. He has written biographies of Curtin, *John Curtin: A life* (1999) and *Chifley* (2002).

Peter Edwards, AM, is a Visiting Professor at the University of New South Wales, Australian Defence Force Academy, Canberra. His biography of Sir Arthur Tange, *Arthur Tange: Last of the mandarins*, was published in 2006.

Ian Hancock is a Visiting Fellow at the Australian Dictionary of Biography, at The Australian National University. His book, *John Gorton: He did it his way*, was published in 2002.

John Nethercote is the Consulting Editor of the *Australian Journal of Public Administration*. He has written obituaries of several senior Commonwealth officials, including Sir Frederick Wheeler, Dr H. C. Coombs, Dr Peter Wilenski, Sir John Bunting and Sir Allen Brown.

Rod (R.A.W.) Rhodes is Professor of Political Science and Head of Program in the Political Science Program, Research School of Social Sciences, The Australian National University. He is author, with Mark Bevir, of *Governance Stories* (2005) and *Interpreting British Governance* (2003). And, with Patrick Weller, *The Changing World of Top Officials: Mandarins or valets?* (2001).

Tim Rowse is Professor of History in the Research School of Social Sciences, The Australian National University. He wrote *Obliged to be Difficult* (2000) and *Nugget Coombs: A reforming life* (2002).

Philip Selth is Executive Director of the New South Wales Bar Association. He was formerly a senior executive in the Commonwealth, State and Territory sectors, and is an avid reader of political biographies.

James Walter is Professor of Political Science in the School of Political and Social Inquiry at Monash University, Victoria. He has published widely on Australian politics, history, biography and culture. Among his books are *The Leader: A political biography of Gough Whitlam* (1980) and *The Ministers' Minders: Personal advisers in national government* (1986).

Rae Wear is a Senior Lecturer in Political Science at the University of Queensland. She wrote *Johannes Bjelke-Petersen: the Lord's Premier*, published in 2002. She is Associate Editor of the *Australian Journal of Politics and History* and previously taught at the University of Southern Queensland.

Patrick Weller, AO, is Professor and Director of the Centre for Governance and Public Policy at Griffith University, Queensland. He is the author of *Don't Tell the Prime Minister* (2002), *Australia's Mandarins: The frank and the fearless* (2001), *Malcolm Fraser PM* (1989) and *Dodging Raindrops* (1999).

Preface

Political biography is a window to a previous world of political practice. From this window, we see politics through the eyes and experiences of an individual subject. We follow their actions and inactions, see their behaviour, experience their world from afar. Often we are treated to insider stories — their observations, reflections, understandings, and motivations. We read events from their vantage point or interpretations. Biography is the celebration of the personalised account.

Many biographies and autobiographies have been written about or by leading figures in government and politics. In particular, the last decade of the twentieth century — as the century of the Federation approached — witnessed a spate of biographies of Australian political figures and, in a couple of cases, even senior administrative figures. Australian prime ministers figure prominently as subjects although only a few have composed memoirs or penned accounts of major events in which they were involved. Other political and governmental personalities at both the national and state level have also featured prominently this emerging literature. A few ministers have written autobiographical accounts and a small number at the national level themselves have been subjects of biography. But there the trail tends to turn cold.

Those undertaking the task of biography, the biographers, have typically been historians, political scientists or journalists. In choosing historical subjects, their motivations have occasionally been some distant knowledge of the subject or the times in which they lived, but, where the subject is still alive or only recently dead, there it is often some personal factor that draws the biographer to the task. Most, but not all, have a sympathy for their chosen subject. They usually furnish a largely favourable portrait. Herein lies the ambivalence of the genre.

Political biography sometimes sits uncomfortably with the more conventional writing and scholarship on politics and political science. It is often regarded as 'less academic', overly subjective, and too partial. It does not appear 'explanatory' in orientation or theoretical in approach; it does not articulate a rigorous methodology shared by likeminded scholars. It is sometimes not even regarded as quite kosher; its standing as proper scholarship may even be suspect. Some biographers are not regarded as part of the 'academic club' or belong only at the margins.

Nevertheless, biographies (and autobiographies) have much to offer the student of politics. Political biography is an alternative narrative of events — a personalised view stressing the familiar and the specific. It contributes the views of political actors — sometimes in a contemporary context, sometimes with the benefit of hindsight. It can reinforce existing accounts of events or produce new accounts. It can add new perspectives and insights to existing accounts. It provides a medium through which the personal 'take' on politics is able to be 'written in' to conventional accounts. Crucially, political biographies are often the most accessible and widely read form of political writing, attracting readerships beyond the purely scholarly interest or the political junkie market. We recognise 'good biographies' and praise them for their contribution to knowledge. We regard them as essential reading to give depth and flavour to political actors, or to provide a sense of urgency or poignancy to political events.

Accordingly, it was timely to convene a workshop on political biography and administrative histories, to survey the field and appraise the achievements. It took place at University House in The Australian National University in May 2005. Interest ranged from the purpose and role of biography, the choice of subject, methodologies of and obstacles to research, and the style and structure of the book itself. The workshop provided a means of prompting biographers from a range of disciplinary backgrounds to reflect on their craft and to consider how this form of research contributes to the study of government and politics. We intentionally invited participants who had made contributions from a wide range of biographical traditions: historical and political biographies, studies of political leaders, biographies of influential but non-elected figures, biographies of administrators, autobiographies and memoirs of key practitioners.

This monograph thus brings together some of the best practitioners of the art and craft of political biography in Australia. They are simultaneously some of our best scholars who, at least in part, have turned their attention to writing Australian political lives. They are not merely chroniclers of our times but multidisciplinary analysts constructing layers of explanation and theoretical insight. They include academic, professional and amateur biographers; scholars from a range of disciplines (politics, history, sociology, public administration, gender studies); and politicians who for a time strutted the political stage. The assembled papers explore the strengths and weaknesses of the biographical approach; the enjoyment it can deliver; the problems and frustrations of writing biographies; and the various ways the 'project' can be approached by those constructing these lives. They probe the art and craft of the political biographer.

The workshop was organised by Tracey Arklay and John Wanna with the support of the Australia and New Zealand School of Government. Tracey Arklay is herself engaged in doctoral research for a biography of Sir Arthur Fadden, leader of the Country Party from 1940 to 1958 and Prime Minister of Australia in 1941. John Nethercote and John Wanna assisted her in preparing the papers presented at the workshop for publication in this volume. At a later stage, John Butcher assisted in copyediting and oversaw the finalisation of the text. We would like to thank those who helped in the organisation of the event — especially Patrick Weller from the Centre for Governance and Public Policy at Griffith University who assisted with funding the workshop, and Mary Hapel, Jenny Keene and Rod Rhodes from the ANU. We are indebted to many others who attended the workshop as participants and gave generously of their time, comments and experience — those we would like to acknowledge who are not included in this volume are: Jenni Craik, Derek Drinkwater, James Mathews, Brendon O'Connor, Andrew Podger and Anne Tiernan.

Tracey Arklay, John Nethercote and John Wanna
Griffith University and The Australian National University
July 2006

The Art of Australian Political Biography

Geoffrey Bolton

Real intellectuals do not do political biography. Biography as a genre is suspect because it lends itself to a discourse of old fashioned narrative, beginning with the life and parentage of the subject and heading predictably towards death and posthumous reputation. Political biography is doubly suspect because it carries with it a whiff of the 'great man in history' heresy. This suggests that if Halifax and not Churchill had become prime minister of Britain in 1940, or if Al Gore had won the presidential elections in the United States in 2000, the world somehow would not have been absolutely identical to the world we know today. Political biography, at least since Plutarch nearly two thousand years ago, is also prone to contamination with a moral agenda, or at the very least to an implication that the lives of past statesmen may convey lessons and examples to the political leaders of our own generation. (And my use of the term 'statesman' will alert the perceptive reader to the further danger that, since individuals of the masculine persuasion have traditionally exercised political power, political biography is ineradicably flawed with gender bias.)

So it is that the practitioner of political biography may be compared to an old-fashioned craftsman in an Alpine village laboriously carving cuckoo clocks by time-honoured methods, while in the big town in the valley below the Swatch factory is turning out bright new up-to-the-minute products replete with every new device fresh from the laboratories of culture studies and post-modernism. Yet, curiously, political biography survives. Even the most transient and mediocre of American presidents is embalmed in a mausoleum of four, five, or six fat volumes, with a library of presidential papers the pride and joy of his home town campus.

The monuments of British prime ministers are hardly smaller. Churchill lies entombed in the million words of the official eight volume biography by Randolph S. Churchill and Sir Martin Gilbert (1966-88), though I have yet to meet the brave soul who could swear, hand on heart, to have read every word. Most would prefer the mercifully succinct account and the practical insights provided by another veteran of the House of Commons, Roy Jenkins (2001). Macmillan, surprisingly for a man of his wit and presence, erected his own grey six-volume cenotaph (1966-1973). Australian political biography as yet may claim to be fairly free of such gigantism. Even two volume biographies, such as La Nauze on Alfred Deakin (1965), Fitzhardinge on Hughes (1964; 1979) or Allan

Martin on Menzies (1993; 1999), present themselves apologetically, although their subjects were pre-eminent in their generation.

It is therefore with a sense of taking the easy option that I state that this essay intends to confine itself to Australian political biography, and specifically to the biography of politicians since introduction of responsible government in the middle of the nineteenth century. The lives of the founding governors, Phillip and Macquarie, Arthur and Franklin, Stirling and La Trobe, raised different questions within a different context of imperial administration. I intend to chart selectively the development of political biography in Australian historiography, concentrating on examples which throw light on three questions:

- The self-consciousness or otherwise with which political figures concern themselves with their reputation in the eyes of posterity and take care to shape the record accordingly.
- The extent to which the public career of a political leader may be satisfactorily analysed with exploration into the inner recesses of his or her private life.
- The survival of Plutarch's ghost or, in other words, the political biographer's temptation to write about a deceased politician as commentary on the politics of the present day.

These are all questions of immediate relevance to myself, since I am engaged on a biography of Sir Paul Hasluck and find myself confronted with each of them.

Sir Henry Parkes was the nineteenth century politician most obviously aware of his own place in history. This became plain during the centenary celebrations for New South Wales in 1888. His proposal that Centennial Park should become the site for a national mausoleum for eminent Australians foundered, among other reasons, on the suspicion that the 73-year-old premier had his own agenda about who might be among its first occupants. Parkes went on to publish his autobiographical *50 Years in the Making of Australian History*, and at his death in 1896 he became almost immediately the subject of a biography by Charles Lyne. Undoubtedly Parkes looked over his shoulder at the reputation won by his exact contemporary, Sir John A. Macdonald, as architect of Canadian confederation, with whom he was sometimes compared. But despite the generous tributes paid to Parkes when federation was achieved in 1901, and despite his early recognition when the first precincts in Canberra were named, there was no move for a more considered account of his career than Charles Lyne's. Perhaps he was seen as too exclusively a New South Wales identity; perhaps his marital history was an embarrassment; perhaps it was simply that in the early twentieth century Australian historical writing was mainly bound up with exploration and settlement, and politicians possessed less appeal.

From time to time during the 1920s an obituary volume appeared commemorating a State politician — H. C. Perry on Sir Robert Philp, for instance, or Sugden and

Eggleston (1931) on George Swinburne, but their reception was modest. Perhaps neither was seen as a figure quite of the first order. It might have been thought that the making of the Australian Commonwealth would provide a stimulus for nationalist biographers, especially after death claimed so many of the founders — Barton, Reid, Deakin, Griffith, Forrest, Fysh — in a sweep between 1918 and 1920. This, however, was slow in coming.

Barton was sufficiently aware of his place in history to spend a considerable amount of time with his wife in destroying those parts of their correspondence which they did not wish to remain on the public record, though fortunately for the historian they were not entirely thorough. Deakin, as so often the most systematic of them all, kept orderly newspaper cuttings and correspondence. In his retirement, despite his gathering decrepitude, he went through his diaries and identified those entries which he judged of greatest historical significance. When I was writing my biography of Barton, I thought seriously of acknowledging his usefulness as a research assistant.

His family commissioned Walter Murdoch to write a biographical work about him within a few years of his death. Murdoch, already an admirer, produced a portrait (1923) which tended to entrench the Victorian view of Deakin as the main architect of Federation, and thus implicitly to play down the importance of Barton as broker of consensus or Reid as the canny bargainer who ensured the essential presence of New South Wales in the Commonwealth. Because of the later pre-eminence of Melbourne in the production of Australian history this view has dominated Australian historiography. One would not wish to over-compensate by removing Deakin from his pedestal, but his reputation stands as reminder to statesmen to bequeath orderly archives to appreciative historians. By the end of the 1920s the National Library of Australia was starting to establish itself as the receptacle for manuscript collections of potential historical importance. The Barton archives was one of the first collections to find its way there and Deakin's papers followed before long.

Federation as a sustaining myth for Australian materialism was eclipsed during the 1920s and 1930s by the story of ANZAC and the *Official History of Australia in the War of 1914-1918* as edited by Charles Bean stressed the part played by the rank and file rather than the achievements of individual generals. Another discourse which might lend itself to political biography could be found in the history of the Australian Labor movement, though the splits of 1916 and 1931 made it hard to identify figures who could be seen as sustaining Labor ideals throughout their lives. Dr H. V. Evatt, whose importance in Australian historiography has been overshadowed by his controversial political record, tackled these issues.

Evatt's first excursion into the field, *The Rum Rebellion,* is admittedly little better than a defence counsel's argument in favour of Captain William Bligh, to whom in some respects Evatt himself bore an uncanny resemblance. But in 1940 he produced *Australian Labour Leader: The story of W.A. Holman and the labour movement,* a biography of a hero of his youth, William Holman, who had seemed a brilliant State premier before the conscription crisis drew him into the Nationalist ranks in 1916-17. Evatt's biography is too long, and it has its indulgent moments, as when he introduces several political ditties from the Sydney University students, which he very probably wrote himself, but after more than sixty years it has yet to be supplanted. Knowing that in the early years of the Second World War Evatt, then a newcomer in federal politics, played with the concept of an all-party coalition. The question arises as to whether he regarded Holman as an example or a warning.

It was to be twenty years before a similarly significant biography of a Labor leader was to be produced. When L. F. Crisp published *Ben Chifley* in 1961 its underlying agenda was very different. Chifley as wartime Treasurer, and as Prime Minister from 1945 to 1949, had been a major architect, if not the major architect, of post-war reconstruction and the creation of a policy which placed full employment and access to social opportunity foremost among its goals. Most of these goals were sustained by the Menzies Coalition government after 1949, but the Federal Labor party under Evatt disintegrated into schism and what seemed an eternity in opposition. Crisp and several others who had been prominent young standard bearers of post-war reconstruction in administrative positions under Chifley found refuge in Canberra University College and in the Australian National University. In the late 1950s and early 1960s they resembled a little colony of Jacobite exiles hoping against hope that the King would come into his own.

Crisp presented Chifley as a sagacious and practical statesman, almost without fault, whose vision Labor needed to recover. Chifley had served the nation well while remaining faithful to his party and its principles, but a feckless electorate beguiled by the promise of consumer goods and an end to rationing had failed to appreciate his quality. So Crisp hoped to keep aglow the light on the hill during the barren years of opposition. It was a very good biography, but it might have been even better with a little more shade to the light, and it had one surprising omission. Late in his research Crisp discovered that in the 1920s Chifley went overseas for the first time, working his passage on a steamship to South Asia to observe conditions there at first hand. Unaccountably he decided to ignore this episode though it would have enhanced Chifley's reputation for foresight and concern for social justice.

Crisp published in 1961 at a moment when The Australian National University had recently taken probably the most momentous step to promote biography in the history of Australian scholarship. Inspired by L. F. Fitzhardinge and energised by Sir Keith Hancock, the production of the *Australian Dictionary of Biography* grew into a unique example of major co-operative humanities research which has endured for nearly half a century. Its importance for the writing of political biography lay partly in the dozens of essays on political figures commissioned for its seventeen volumes, ranging from the numerous 500 word sketches of third-order parliamentarians to the 5000 or 6000 words required for heavyweights such as Menzies or Evatt. At their best these articles, drafted in conformity with the house style of the *ADB,* attain the simple perfection of a haiku or a sonnet; Geoffrey Serle's studies of major and minor worthies of late nineteenth century Victoria are elegant masterpieces, and would probably repay anthologising. These articles in turn created a bank of research data that could be quarried by authors seeking to write about an individual at greater depth. In some cases also, *ADB* articles stimulated authors to go on to attempt a full scale biography, or at the very least enabled authors with a full-scale work in their sights, such as Allan Martin with Henry Parkes, to rehearse the arguments and explore the issues which they proposed exploring in greater depth.

Within The Australian National University, Laurie Fitzhardinge with W. M. Hughes (1964; 1979) and John La Nauze with Deakin (1965) set high standards of political biography, though in each case it could be argued that they scored higher in treating their subject's public character than in understanding their private personalities. An old-fashioned gentlemanly reticence may have restrained Fitzhardinge from some revelations, but it is surely relevant that in old age Hughes confessed to the diplomat Malcolm Booker (who later published it in his own biography) that, as a scrawny young new chum knocking around the back blocks of Queensland, he (Hughes) lived in fear of homosexual rape. This must throw light on Hughes's attitude to the possession and use of power in a Hobbesian world of potential violence. Hughes was also an unsatisfactory family man, who more or less repudiated the six children of his first, probably de facto wife, of whom Fitzhardinge makes brief mention, and who behaved badly over the death in illegitimate childbirth of the daughter by his second marriage — about which Fitzhardinge must almost certainly have known more than he wrote. I shall return to this issue of the interface between private and public life later.

La Nauze could convincingly describe Deakin as a devoted husband and parent, and faced no such dilemma. He was, however, temperamentally unsuited to sympathetic explanation of Deakin's mystical streak, at one point wryly commenting that the young man would have been better off playing cricket than pondering over Swendenborgian metaphysics. It was left to Al Gabay (1992) to make good the omission in a monograph which largely confines itself to Deakin the mystic without exploring very far the implications for his political life. For the biographer there remains a problem of reconciling Deakin's preoccupation with ethical standards with his capacity to inspire mistrust in many of his contemporaries. When Hughes attacked Deakin as one who had joined all parties and betrayed all parties, it may have been a cheap shot, but there was a sting in it appreciated by many. Blunt Sir John Forrest after a long association decided that Deakin was not a safe man to go tiger-shooting with. And in our own time Frank Crowley has commented on the paradox of a senior Commonwealth cabinet minister accepting pay from a conservative London daily (the *Morning Post*) for anonymous articles about Australian affairs. In these Deakin affected the persona of one who was sometimes quite critical of the policies of the Federal ministry. Some of the subtleties in 'Affable Alfred' remain to be teased out.

Not all the interactions between private and public characters were necessarily scandalous or contentious. It was, for instance, a strength of Crisp's account of Chifley when he noted that for several years in his boyhood Chifley was sent away from his parents and two younger brothers to live with a rather taciturn and solitary widowed grandfather. Crisp could legitimately argue that this experience helped to shape Ben Chifley into the self-reliant but not particularly gregarious adult in public life.

Some biographers have wondered if use might be made of the insights of psychology and psychotherapy as a systematic aid to the explanation of historical character. Martin for a time was attracted by the ideas of Erik Erikson (1959), who postulated that emotional growth through a human lifetime depended on successfully confronting eight developmental crises at different points in the life-cycle. Although traces of his approach lingered in the final version of his biography of Parkes, Martin came largely to discard Erikson's model in favour of a more empirical approach to the evidence. Little trace of it may be found in his later two-volume life of Menzies, but it may still be that the questions Martin put to his source materials were sharpened by acquaintance with Erikson's theories.

James Walter (1980) has made the most thorough application of psychological theory to biography in his study of Gough Whitlam, *The Leader*. Many of his findings are valid and plausible, but debate will inevitably continue as to whether a different historian without theoretical foundations might have arrived at very similar conclusions through observation of available evidence. In recent years there seem to have been fewer examples of the conscious use of psychological theory as a biographical tool. Recent attempts by North American and British historians to plot family history by using the concept of *genograms* — models in which patterns of behaviour are shown to have a tendency to replicate themselves over several generations — have not to my knowledge been widely attempted in Australia. But perhaps Joy Damousi's recent *Freud in the Antipodes* (2001), describing the growth of psychoanalytical thought in twentieth century Australia, will turn scholarly inquiry once more to the possible nexus between psychoanalysis and biography. If so, due attention must be paid to the difficulty of transferring the psychotherapeutic techniques used with a living client to the understanding of a dead politician.

This question of the interface between private and public character keeps coming back to me in attempting the biography of Paul Hasluck. At the most obvious it lies in the widely held perception that there was a striking disjunction between his private self and the persona which he presented in ministerial office. The contrast was, in the words of one who knew him, 'schizophrenic'. The public Hasluck was seen as aloof, pedantic, demanding, censorious, a hard and often unappreciative taskmaster. It was notorious that at the January 1968 contest for the party leadership, in contrast to the energetic campaigning of Gorton and the frenetic lobbying of McMahon to retain the deputy leadership, Hasluck remained aloof, not even engaging in casual party room conversation on the morning of the election. By contrast, there is equally wide testimony that the private Hasluck was warm, hospitable, and considerate, an intelligent and lively minded conversationalist but one who was perhaps never happier than when yarning with the stockmen at a bush camp.

He belonged to a generation who set greater store than our own on formal behaviour in public, but there is not the same sense of contrast between the public and private personas in Menzies or Chifley or Evatt or McEwen. There is a recognisable continuum between the personality on or off duty. Hasluck's administrative style can be readily explained as a reaction against his five years working under Evatt as minister, with his erratic and chaotic business habits, his suspiciousness, his readiness to play favourites. But is that sufficient explanation requiring no exploration of the private man?

Another perplexing facet of Hasluck's personality lies in what might be called his 'Prince Hal' syndrome, his tendency to turn away from and repudiate activities in which he had seemed deeply engaged. He was a pioneer oral historian as a young man in Western Australia. His interviews with elderly pioneers, taken in Pitman's shorthand and subsequently typed up, offer uniquely valuable insights into the first and second generations of settlers in the mid-nineteenth century colony. As late as 1948, when he was researching for his volumes of the *Official History of Australia in the Second World War* (1952; 1970), he could write to Robert Menzies that 'the unrecorded pages of history … could only be written down from the memory of those who took part'. But in later years he disparaged oral history as subjective and unreliable. He was a proficient journalist, apparently popular with his fellow journalists, but as a politician he could be scathing about the profession. He was a respected officer of the Department of External Affairs in the 1940s, but his comments about diplomats and the public service in old age are seldom flattering. He led the life of politics for eighteen years but his judgments of his colleagues in *The Chance of Politics* (1997) — and that book is an edited selection from which the most wounding comments have been left out — are perceived by not a few readers as harsh. He was no more sparing of himself than he was of other people. From where did this come, this inability to be satisfied?

Here the practice of other biographers may be helpful. But some, such as Tim Rowse in writing about H. C. Coombs, have adopted a self-denying ordinance about exploring their subject's private life. Deference to the feelings of people still living may call for such reticence, and a skilful historian or biographer can often use the public record to arrive at conclusions compatible with what is known but not stated about the private record. There is nevertheless disappointment when, in a generally lively and informative study of the first Labor prime minister, Chris Watson, Ross McMullin (2004) tersely informs us that Watson's premature retirement from federal politics was due to his wife's complaints about his frequent absences from home in Sydney. One would never know that Watson's concern for his wife arose partly because his presence helped her in a battle against alcoholism, nor that after her death he re-married and somewhat belatedly found fulfilment as a parent. As I say, this does not detract from the quality of McMullin's assessment of Watson's public career, but is more required of a biographer?

Where private experience is presented as shaping a public persona it is often the experience of childhood and adolescence which serves as evidence. Crisp's account of Chifley's isolated childhood is one such case. The discovery by Chris Cunneen (2000) that William McKell's father deserted his family and went off to that land of bigamous opportunity, Western Australia, is another, since the responsibility thrust upon the eldest boy of the family helped to shape the attributes and political beliefs of the adult William McKell. David Day is one of the few recent political biographers to attempt to chart the interface between an adult politician's public and private lives, and this is commendable, but in my view the results are uneven. He shows convincingly that Curtin's battle against alcoholism was more protracted than has previously been supposed, and that his ultimate break with the booze was not as clear-cut as other writers made it out to be; but ultimately Curtin's defeat of his demons is more credible as a result.

On the other hand, I am not quite convinced by Day's effort to show that Chifley's relationship with his secretary, Phyllis Donnelly, was actively sexual. Duncan Waterson's tactful phrase, 'affectionate friend', suggests a surer sense of nuance. The world of Chifley's generation contained numerous examples of secretaries who became 'office wives', women whose potential husbands were killed in the First World War. They devoted themselves loyally to their boss, fetched and carried for him, protected his privacy, brought order into his working life, and sought no career outside his service. Sometimes, as Ross Fitzgerald (1994) shows in his life of E. G. Theodore, the employer's wife became jealous of the secretary's emotional closeness. Sometimes, as with Sir John McEwen, he married his secretary after his first wife died. But in the generation of Chifley and Phyllis Donnelly, both products of Catholic culture, desires often remained unacted. We must not bring anachronistic expectations to bear.

When I wrote about Edmund Barton, I found that his sexual and emotional life, like much of his personality, was relatively uncomplicated. He fell in love at the age of twenty-one, courted Jeanne Ross patiently for seven years until they could afford to marry, and lived happily ever after despite debts and frequent absences from home until he achieved the financial security of a seat on the High Court bench. The problem about Barton lay in his notorious reputation for indolence contrasting with his demonstrably hard work at the two federal conventions. His medically qualified grandson, David Barton, wrote to me that Edmund's behaviour was bi-polar in origin, so that in periods of depression he indeed found solace in food, drink and inactivity, while at other times he could draw on reserves of concentrated energy. This was a hypothesis for which I had not been able to find any contemporary recognition, but a medical opinion buttressed by the weight of family authority was good enough.

Guided by this insight, it was possible to identify two periods in Barton's life when after a period of strenuous activity and pressure he had lapsed into the lethargy and overindulgence of which critics complained. In 1893, having survived the Broken Hill strike and the threatened collapse of the banking system, he was overtaken by a crisis in his personal finances, and fell into the pattern of overeating and drinking as a symptom of depression. His perceptive premier, Dibbs, sent him with his wife on a government-funded sea cruise and recovery followed. In the early months of 1902, after the achievement of Federation and the crowded first session of Federal Parliament, living away from home in makeshift quarters, he underwent another bout. His friends and colleagues, Alfred Deakin and Richard O'Connor, had to cover for him, and this episode understandably coloured Deakin's recollections of Barton, and hence the assessments of later historians relying on Deakin as a source. The health of the private Barton influenced his public performance and hence the judgment of historians and biographers coming later.

My question about the extent to which politicians are conscious of the verdict of posterity, and take care that the record shows them in a favourable light may not reflect a widespread problem. Biographers are probably more often exasperated by the failure of their subject to leave adequate evidence. With Paul Hasluck, however, we are dealing with a man who was already a good historian before he became a politician and cabinet minister. He was acutely aware of the demands of the historical record. It is not just that in retirement he published several substantial books reflecting on aspects of his public career. The possibility remains that during more than seventeen years in a diligent ministerial career every minute which he penned on a departmental submission, every submission carried to cabinet, was written in expectation of the scrutiny of the future.

This is a different problem from the more usual one of coping with the rationalisations and self-justifications which appear in the autobiographies written by politicians after their retirement (though some of these personal accounts, such as those by Bill Hayden and Neal Blewett, make useful contributions to the understanding of their period). It is different again from the challenge inherent in reading Don Watson's *Memoirs of a Bleeding Heart* (2002), a work that is neither quite autobiography nor quite biography. No future biographer of Paul Keating will be able to escape the shaping influence of Watson's account, written as it is with immediacy and insight. It is not just a matter of commemorating the style and content of Keating's administration and perhaps contrasting it with the cautious and measured pragmatism of Keating's successor. Because Watson is less adulatory of Keating than Crisp was of Chifley, he may be acquitted of writing a tract to hearten the faithful during the long years of opposition. But he has to some extent given a decisive turn to future historiography, and no doubt he intended to do so.

In Australia we are immediately up against the tendency of the general public to believe that the politicians of their youth were figures of greater stature than the pygmies in public life today. Howard and Beazley are no match for Fraser and Whitlam; but twenty years ago Curtin, Chifley and Menzies were extolled as Australia's greatest prime ministers. Only an ancient like myself can remember that in their years of office they were often compared unfavourably with the likes of Deakin and Fisher and Hughes. Sometimes it is the misfortune of a politician to become associated with causes which are currently out of fashion. George Reid, for example, could be seen as a lonely anachronism in espousing free trade in an era of liberal protectionism. He was further ill-served by Deakin's pen-portraits of him as little more than an artful buffoon, but W. G. McMinn's biography (1989) put paid to that stereotype. Now that tariff protection is no longer in favour and free trade in the form of globalisation is the dominant orthodoxy, Reid is in the process of resurrection as a harbinger of social policy. In like manner Henry Reynolds has rehabilitated Bruce Smith, previously dismissed as a spokesman for employers who wanted to introduce cheap non-European labour into White Australia, as a tolerant multiculturalist ahead of his time. The fluctuations of the biographical stock market are fascinating.

For me these questions arise insistently in the case of Hasluck, since he was deeply implicated in two seriously contentious issues: the shaping of Aboriginal policy and Australia's involvement in the Vietnam war. Hasluck's involvement in Aboriginal policy puts me in mind of Lord Melbourne's cynical aphorism: 'You had better try to do no good, and then you'll get into no scrapes'. In the 1930s and 1940s Hasluck was one of the earliest advocates of a better deal for Australian Aborigines, his first major publication *Black Australians* (1942) breaking the great Australian silence that had largely written them out of the history books. In twelve years as Minister for Territories, from 1951 to 1963, he did much to influence Aboriginal policy, and as a result now stands condemned by many as the apparent architect of the policy of removing Aboriginal children from their parents. Some passages of the *Bringing them Home* report[1] may be read as implying this, but Hasluck only endorsed the practice as a last resort.

The situation has not been helped by historians such as Geoffrey Partington (1996) who have set Hasluck up as a wise paternalist contrasted with his contemporary Coombs and his quixotic ideals of Aboriginal autonomy. It is relevant that Hasluck's main impact on policy came in the 1950s, when it was possible to hope that Aborigines, especially in northern Australia, might find employment not only in the traditional pastoral industry but through agriculture, mining and forestry without disruption to their culture. Coombs came to Aboriginal policy in the late 1960s, by which time Aborigines had been displaced from the cattle stations and new social problems had arisen for which solutions were needed. In assessing both men, a biographer in the early twenty-first century must sedulously avoid applying the insights and criteria of today.

Similarly with the Vietnam war. The thirtieth anniversary of the fall of Saigon has brought forward revisionists justifying the American intervention and therefore the Australian participation in that conflict. Within Australia a school of historians beginning with Michael Sexton (1981) and Greg Pemberton (2002) have portrayed Australia as the willing tool of the Americans, even as goading-on Washington to greater intervention. In the current state of my research I find that in the year preceding Australia's decision of April 1965, which was Hasluck's first year as Minister for External Affairs, there was often a perplexed lack of clarity in Canberra about American intentions. Hasluck, indeed, insisted to his colleagues that Vietnam was a more serious problem for Australian security than the confrontation between Indonesia and Malaysia, but when Menzies decided that Australian troops should be sent to Vietnam, Hasluck demurred and unavailingly suggested caution. (It must have irked him that his only ally among senior cabinet ministers was McMahon, whom he despised.) It is my hope that a Hasluck biography may encourage a more nuanced approach in the writing of the recent general history of Australia.

In his report on the National Museum of Australia John Carroll (2003) suggested that its historical section should give greater salience to Australian heroes (he weakened his case by including among his examples Burke and Wills, surely the most tragically incompetent of explorers.) There will always be a public appetite for heroes and villains, Ned Kelly against Sir Redmond Barry, but this is not the proper business of historians and biographers. Political biographers in particular must learn to live with ambiguity, and to learn to present their materials skilfully enough to persuade their readers to accept ambiguity. Actors in politics such as Parkes or Barton or Curtin may live much of their careers in the same mundane and contradictory muddle as the rest of us without losing the capacity to touch greatness in a moment of crisis, or at other moments to fall below their best. With all respect to John Carroll I find greater wisdom in that aphorism of Bertolt Brecht: 'Happy is the land that has no need of heroes'.

ENDNOTES

[1] Human Rights and Equal Opportunity Commission (1997). *Bringing them home: report of the National Inquiry into the Separation of Aboriginal and Torres Strait Islander Children from their Families*, (Commonly known as *Stolen children report* or *Stolen generations report*) Parliamentary paper no. 128.

Political Biography: Its Contribution to Political Science

Tracey Arklay

In Australia we rely on journalists to give the 'first draft' of history, chronicling people and events. Often immediate, spontaneous, exciting, seeking impact, what is reported is frequently the sexiest and occasionally the most sordid aspects of accounts and personalities. Such newspaper articles, for example, usually have a narrative structure; there is less analysis of 'why and how'. The research undertaken for media accounts is rarely 'triangulated'. [1] More reflective comment on why an event occurred or why a person acted in a particular way may well be lost in the ensuing debate. For journalists, a week is a long time in politics (in the words of the former British Prime Minister, Harold Wilson). This is in contrast to the time-line of biographers, who may take years and sometimes decades to complete their account of a subject's life. Journalists and biographers use different research methods and different sets of skills.

With the benefit of hindsight, journalistic reports, which are necessarily speedily written, may prove inaccurate and lack the balance that develops with the luxury of time. The price of the luxury of time is, however, usually loss of nuance. With controversial figures such as Gough Whitlam, for example, accounts of his brief and tumultuous time in office were either negative or positive. Whitlam was seen either as hero or villain (Walter 1997: 28). Malcolm Fraser, too, was accorded either a reluctant hero or departed demon status depending on which side of the political fence you sat (Weller 1989:xii). The political consequences of actions take longer to be felt, absorbed and filtered. Some journalists have become acclaimed historians/biographers in their own right. Paul Kelly, Michelle Grattan, Shaun Carney and David Marr are among those Australian journalists who continue to provide readers with an insight into how federal politics and its actors work through books as well as articles (see Weller 2005).

Biography is a very old form of political writing. Suetonius (1957) chronicled the lives of a selected number of 'great men', from Julius Caesar to Domitian, in his sensationalist Twelve Caesars. Plutarch's biographical studies, Parallel Lives, provided readers with an insight into the political events of classical Greece and Rome. His contrasting Greek and Roman personalities have long been heralded as a 'unique example of the genre of biography in the ancient world'. [2] Despite its long history, political biography as a genre remains under-appreciated and controversial – sometimes evoking palpable hostility among intellectuals who have argued that the form may be literary, but that it is not history (O'Brien, cited in Pimlott 1999). Critics of political biography note the marginal impact of most individuals on big events. While political biography as part of mainstream political science is becoming better appreciated, there are still debates about the appropriateness of certain methodologies (see Brett 1997: vii).

This essay examines the genre of political biography. First, it defines what biography is or attempts to be. Second, it explores the different forms biography can take and the methodological approaches used in biography. It then reviews the contribution biographical study makes to political science and reviews the criticisms that have been made of the method. It concludes with an explanation of some of the problems encountered by writers attempting to re-create a life.

What is biography?

A simple definition of biography is that it is 'an account of a person's life written, composed, or produced by another'. [3] Political biography is the form through which writers breathe life into archival documents such as letters and diaries, birth, death and marriage certificates, Hansard and official records, to assist in the re-creation of a life. To the criticism that biography is a means by which we get a chance to 'play God', biography, through utilising the rich information contained in yellowed relics of another era, can provide insights that are built upon by the writer. As Pimlott (1999:34) stated, 'the most exciting aspect of biography is that it links together human events in the way human beings actually experience them'. Biography should never be viewed as a tool by which to make universal sense of a subject. It is a subjective and highly interpretative method, one in which seeking the 'compassionate truth' should never be underplayed.

Biography is not simple reportage of one life (Pimlott 1985: xi), nor is it merely a narrative. It certainly cannot hope and should not pretend to be the whole truth. The method is historical, interpretive and, like much social science research, the implicit motivations drawn out in biography are frequently hard to test and often difficult to quantify. It is therefore selective and open to critique. Frequently, as is the case with L.F. Crisp's 1961 life of Ben Chifley and, three and a half decades later, David Day's Chifley, biographical research builds upon what has been uncovered by another. They can, thus, be viewed as 'works in progress,' progressively enhancing what is known about a subject as an increasingly detailed portrait emerges. It is questionable as to whether there is any such thing as a definitive biography. Some biographies, however, are indispensable and some of such quality that it is unlikely they will be superseded subsequently.

A challenge in writing about a life is acknowledging and processing the changes made during that life — personally, professionally and spiritually. Studies that focus on a person within a time-frame (for example, as prime minister only), and ignore other periods, are in danger of over-simplification. A.W. Martin, in the two volume life of Robert Menzies, had to weave the story of a prime minister who, when he returned for his second term in 1949, was a substantially more mature individual than he had been during his first term (1939-41). How events affect personalities is as important as reflecting on how personalities shape events.

The approaches taken by biographers are varied and include the historical-chronological method, the psycho-analytical method, the historical-novella and the journalistic account. Biography has been defined as a 'dangerous art' (Rickard 1987). It certainly becomes that if the biographer claims to know 'what the person feels' (Tridgell 2004). Historical methodology, the relentless digging up of data to validate the writing of a life, defined by one author as 'rigorous, forensic inquiry', is where the craft of political biography begins (Wheatley 2002). That is the bare minimum. And yet, if political science without biography is, indeed, 'a form of taxidermy' (Lasswell, cited in Walter 1980), why is the methodology of biography on the whole so ill-defined? Many social research method texts do not refer to this form of research explicitly (see, for example, Neuman 1997). Could its popularity be one reason biography, until recently at least, has not rated highly among some academics?[4] Robert Skildelsky, biographer of Oswald Mosely (1975) and John Maynard Keynes (1983-2000), stated the method had 'not yet fully won its intellectual spurs ... as a cogent intellectual enterprise' (cited in Walter (forthcoming)).

Often the method appears as 'art', with amateurs as keen to take up the pen and write the life story of a favourite father, uncle or ancestor. But more prevalent are the thoroughly researched, professionally written, historical accounts which are the focus of this essay. It is here that we find the true craft of writing biography. These works weld the art and the science together. The end result of such writing can provide students of politics with another perspective on how power is wielded and shared, how leaders are made as well as born, and how circumstances can catapult ordinary people into extraordinary situations. Out of the biographical method emerges a set of understandings and contexts that are different from other social science endeavours — of necessity less theoretical and more personal, empathetic and narrative. Narrative research methodology 'directs questions about what it means to interpret and experience the world (rather than explain or predict it)' (Spina and Dodge 2005: 144). It is gaining respect as an approach which can increase our understanding of 'specific phenomena' such as leadership and life experiences of the people under study.[5]

John Dollard wrote in the 1930s about the criteria needed for researching life history.[6] These criteria were established to articulate what he believed should go into the ideal biography. At the forefront was the need to place the individual under study as one member of a social group — which would exist even without our particular subject being born. That provides the context to underpin the notions of where a particular subject fits into history. He urged writers to take account of family influences — where did he/she fit into that grouping of people — the expectations they had of him/her, where was he/she placed in the family as well as the political views held by parents and family and then plot how he/she adapted those views within the context of his own life experiences. Dollard urged writers not to take the subjects own words for this — but triangulate through supporting evidence. Through assessing his/her family's views on broader agendas, writers are then more able to understand the earliest influences on our subject. This provides rudimentary notions of how he/she viewed the world, his/her ideological stance on issues such as, for example, the White Australia policy, communism or sectarianism. For political biographies Dollard suggested two necessary points of reference — the subject's political outlook and his/her style of work in politics (see Davies, 1972).

As Lasswell (cited in Davies 1972: 115) stated, answers to particular questions tell a great deal about the character under study. For example, he suggested the following questions as a tool that would assist researchers in building up a general biographical portrait:

- How does the individual react as a subordinate when confronted by superiors of different kinds (strong and brutal, masterful but objective, weak)?
- How does he act as a superior confronted by subordinates of different kinds (strong, hostile, dangerous rivals; strong and objective; weak)?
- What is his style of expression?
- What is his characteristic mode of thought, and style of decision?
- Is he inventive/ uninventive; quick or slow to suggest policies and tactics; influenced by facts and arguments, appeals to sentiment, personal inducements, sense of public interest, or coercion?
- Does he behave in a traditional style or self-consciously? Does victory or defeat elate or depress him?

Why write biography?

A cynical take on biography is that it serves one of three purposes. First as a hagiography — biography is the standard format used to pay homage to great persons. Political hagiographies are frequently written by partisan persons. For example, the 1997 authorised biography of John Howard, by David Barnett and his wife Pru Goward, was regarded by many as being 'not only a hagiography but a very bad one too' (Switzer 2004:38). Switzer was not alone in his judgment. Alan Ramsey, political columnist of the Sydney Morning Herald, claimed it was not 'only a propagandist's book but a lazy book, too, which could have been written almost entirely from the public record'. The second reason for writing biography, cynics suggest, is to 'set an example for future generations' — Plutarch's various lives are instances of this approach. A final motivation is simply to 'make money' (Gerraty cited in Theakston 2000: 1).

H.B. Higgins, politician and High Court judge, stated that biography was a means by which 'the biographer becomes the disciple, and his temptation to play God, presiding over the subject's life, deftly pulling the strings' is great (Rickard 1987). I could also add biographies are occasionally used as a way of 'getting even'; a method by which to 'discredit a person,' 'expose their failings' or serve as a warning to future generations of what not to do. There are few of these — especially among more recent biographies. Many political biographies in Australia are written by salaried academics. Subjects are selected because they are historically significant and because with biographical research, there always remains the tantalising prospect of what may be uncovered. Many political biographies are funded and written to commemorate significant events — the centenary of the Australian federation, for example. Despite these serious works, the criticisms that have been levelled at the methodology have resulted in political biography being regarded as the 'disciplinary poor relation' to the study of political science more generally (Pimlott 1990:224). As Walter (forthcoming) states:

> The concerns of social scientists with large collectives, mass behaviour, empirical data and testable propositions create difficulties for what are, at best, attempts to link single cases with institutional and historical contexts, and so biography is viewed with scepticism.

Biography and conjecture are a dangerous duo — and raise the question: how much about the life of a person can we hope to know? If biography can tell a life history by 'expos[ing] those intersecting patterns of experience, personality and circumstance which mould a man's response to the contingent and hence lie under the existential surface' (Martin cited in Clendinnen 2004:14), why is it that so many biographers follow the conventional route of chronology? Perhaps because the other is too difficult. The psychoanalytic approach is controversial. While not every biographer sets out to write a psychological style of memoir, Walter is right when he suggested we do need to be aware of patterns of behaviour, how a person reacts under stress — those tell-tale signs — that reveal so much about the subject.

If biography is, as Michael Holroyd, biographer of Lytton Strachey and George Bernard Shaw, stated, a 'cousin to the novel' (Britain 2002:5), then how do you extract meanings from historical facts, archival documents and birth, death and employment records? Biography and memoirs recreate a life. In that regard they use similar 'character-creating techniques' to those used by writers of novels. They are one person's 'take' on another. Seasoned biographers have noted the moral and ethical difficulties inherent in the task. As David Day reflected, after writing a biography of John Curtin, 'it struck me how presumptuous it was for me to be digging around in someone's past life' (Day 2002a). Wheatley (2002) expressed this dilemma another way: he observed that with any person under investigation, the life does not belong to 'readers, or fans, or political supporters ... Most of all ... the life does not belong to the biographer'. A biography in the end is one person's interpretation only.

What does biography add?

Despite the recognition that biography is an incomplete science, biographical research is an 'important way of writing about the past and inspecting the human condition' (Pimlott 1999: 33). Through biographical research, individual experiences and identities can be explored. Biography provides an alternative point of analysis to the workings of social groups, situations and events, which is the normal frame of reference for historical research (see Lieblich et al. 1998: 8). As such it can broaden, rather than reduce, an understanding of who got 'what, when and how' (Lasswell 1970). Academics, critical of biography, argue that traditional historical research reaches a degree of truth and logical explanation for events better than any individual version could hope to do (Carr, cited Pimlott 1999: 32). Yet because biography looks in detail at one of the most micro levels of politics — the individual, the personality and the viewing of events through the lens of one set of eyes — supporters counter that biography could be viewed as a 'neglected' political science methodology that has 'enormous potential for the study of leadership' (Theakston 1997:661). In Australia, most political biographical studies have been on leaders of parties, or of governments (Porter 1993: 1).

Biography contextualises a life but can illuminate much more than just that. Not only is it informative about the person under investigation, it can also tell us much about the person writing the story. Well-written, thoroughly researched studies provide an opportunity to explore issues such as ideology, class struggles and the political machinations within a particular and personal timeframe. It can illustrate the deals, negotiations, horse trading and other compromises that are such an important part of politics. For the personal details, I note Day's recommendation that 'biographers mimic the genealogists and go to the basic sources, such as death certificates, birth certificates, marriage certificates, wills, probate, and employment records' (Day 2002b:36) to lay aside the myths and hyperbole and uncovering the 'fertile facts' that surround public figures — both good and bad (Pimlott 1999).

Author involvement varies depending upon the biographical style selected. Biographies that aim to be objectively written tend to stick close to verifiable facts and demonstrable truths, while the style of the narrative biography comes close to fiction where author interpretation and accounts of imagined conversations based on letters and diaries result in a work that reads more like a historical novel. In fact, all biographical styles use, to a greater or lesser extent, a mixture of these approaches as the author constructs a picture of a person's life from fact and interpretation. One difficulty we are all confronted with is that line that crosses over from writing about what is known to what is unknown.

Questions about why we write biography have several possible answers. The first reason is media and monetarily driven. Biographies about politicians sell well. The second is that biographies provide useful overviews — allowing authors and readers to make connections with people and their history — that might otherwise have been left undiscovered. Finally, political biography can open unexpected doors, allowing researchers to gain new appreciations of past events (Pimlott 1999: 34-5).

What are the problems of writing biography?

Practical problems of biographical research include issues of access and information; length and depth — do we focus, for example, only on a subject's public life? Is it possible to understand this life adequately without taking account of other facets that shape the motives, drives and contexts which make up a human being? If the subject has been previously under-researched, is part of the job of a biographer to make that life interesting or, at least, to find out why the life is interesting? Theakston (2000: 131) noted that biography risks exaggerating a subject's importance. Is it enough to document a public figure because they were there? Readability, reason and relevance — the three R's of writing — are challenges that should not be overlooked. As Wear has argued: 'the task of biography is difficult because it involves sorting through numerous accounts of the subject's career and settling on a final version that imposes order and structure' (Courier-Mail May 17, 2003). Rose (2000: 51) considered that biographers often under-conceptualise their subjects, treating the career of a prime minister as a 'unique set of events, with little or no attempt to plot changes over a period of time longer than the subject's term of office'. I would suggest that biographical writing, after intensive research, can shed light on why events occurred, the reactions of those closest to them, and provide readers with an impression of what life was like within a particular time frame. One example of this is Patrick Weller's *Malcolm Fraser PM*. While the author never claimed this work was a biography, it does nevertheless shed extensive light into Fraser's personality — someone who needed to be in control — and therefore illuminates the character perhaps more than originally intended. The book gives readers an insight into how a leader wielded power through the management and working of executive government.

Choosing a subject

How do biographers choose their subjects? Why do they make the choices they do? David Marr (1980), for example, chose Barwick as a case study, because he did not like or admire him. It seems that his was not an isolated case; Edmund White has noted that 'biography is a form by which little people take revenge on big people' (cited in Britain 2003). Yet Marr admitted that through his examination of Barwick, he ended up having more sympathy for his subject than he expected. Other biographers choose subjects because they knew them intimately — and liked them. Bob Hawke's biographer, Blanche d'Alpuget (1982), is a conspicuous example of this, in that she later became his wife. An earlier instance of a different type is L.F. Crisp's Ben Chifley (1961 — see Day 2002: 39). Tim Rowse (2002) was acquainted with his subject, Nugget Coombs. This led to a work that has been called 'a fine intellectual biography' but one that sheds very little light on the personal side of the subject under study, because of the author's personal promise to the subject under investigation, another reviewer was led to comment, 'a fascinating book, but is it a biography of Coombs?' (Kirby 2002:102; and Nethercote 2002: 104). In the acknowledgments Rowse explains why his biography is very much about the public life of Nugget Coombs:

> Coombs' deposited papers do not include items that reveal what he considered to be his private life ... my consent to Coombs' public/private boundary restrained me from exploring that theme very far. The resulting book is more impersonal than most readers of biographies would wish (Rowse 2002: viii).

Subjectivity, bias and motivations for writing a biography are important considerations when choosing a subject.

Most biographies begin by placing the subject in context. In biographies of politicians this includes an explanation as to why the subject is worthy of further study. For example, one of Geoffrey Bolton's tasks when writing the biography on Edmund Barton was to explain or justify Barton as an important historical figure. Through this sort of engagement, the biographer can find him or herself breaking down the established myths that exist about politicians. In Barton's case this added more substance to the character than was commonly known, for he had earned the reputation of someone who largely enjoyed good food, good wine and convivial company. Bolton's book, by contrast, portrayed Barton as 'the man for the job' — right for his time.

I face a similar challenge in writing a life of Arthur Fadden. Part of the research aims to explore why this individual, Fadden, described as a humorist and as a 'hail fellow well met' type of person, and often largely unnoticed or at best regarded as a bit player in history, is worthy of deeper political analysis. In the case of Arthur Fadden questions about how he maintained a key leadership role for 18 years, some of which were difficult for a still rocky coalition, have so far gone unanswered. He is mentioned in indexes of other books written on the era — once again parodied as a friendly, avuncular figure but with little substance added. Arthur Fadden was elected to the Queensland Legislative Assembly in 1932. He was elected to the House of Representatives in 1936 where he remained for twenty-two years until retirement in 1958. After only four years he was appointed to the coalition ministry and was soon Treasurer. In 1940 Fadden was the compromise candidate who won the leadership of the Country Party, a position he retained for the next eighteen years notwithstanding the presence of such heavyweights as Jack McEwen. In 1941 he became prime minister in his own right following the resignation of Robert Menzies — a position he held for a brief and stormy period until his budget was rejected on the floor of the House of Representatives, the only government to be defeated on its budget. As Leader of the Opposition, 1941-1943, he worked closely with Prime Minister John Curtin and his own successor as Treasurer, Ben Chifley.

In the 1940s Fadden and Menzies forged a working relationship that enabled the coalition parties to emerge as a viable alternative to the Labor Party. In 1949, by way of vigorous campaigning on petrol rationing, and his strident politicking against communism, Fadden was instrumental in securing an electoral victory. He regained the Treasury — the second (and last) Country Party member to head that department.[7] His record as Australia's longest serving Treasurer (around 3620 days) was exceeded for the first time by Treasurer Peter Costello in February 2006.

Political biography provides one set of tools by which to explore history and events from within the temporal and historical context of one life. It allows exploration of the events of history — from a micro perspective — looking at them through the eyes of someone who lived, breathed and was part of that history. No approach is all-embracing. There are difficulties in this methodology. What biographers have — unless they are lucky enough to be working with a live and cooperative subject — are the official records, speeches made, occasional letters deposited in the archives, and personal accounts, mostly written by others. Having a cooperative subject, however, may introduce another set of problems those concerned with hagiography: bias, subjectivity and sometimes even honour. Recent biographies which have been seen to experience these problems are d'Alpuget on Hawke and Barnett & Goward on Howard. Promises made to the live subject are hard to break even in the later event of their death, as Tim Rowse's work on Nugget Coombs exemplifies.

Dead or live subjects?

Paul Hasluck's personal view on biography was that it 'should wait until the subject is dead' (Porter 1993: 4). Judith Brett (1997: 1) refers to the 'task of political biography' which involves telling the story of a life in an intelligible way. When writing a biography of someone who is dead, as in the case of Arthur Fadden, where does the biographer begin to travel down the path of a life and hope to understand it, especially when few contemporaries of the study are still alive? How do we begin to feel like we know, even remotely, someone who leaves few personal records, nor kept any diaries? Dealing with live subjects also poses risks. Walter (1980: xv) refers to image maintenance which is one of the important pieces of political armoury. Studies of live subjects must not be hampered by the subject's natural desire to appear in a favourable light. Even after death, family sensibilities may need to be considered. Sometimes a difficult balancing act ensues between the need to write a truthful account, while at the same time doing the minimum of harm to family reputations. Decisions to include information gleaned about the private lives of public figures will always be controversial.

How to read between the lines?

When writing a biography of a political figure there are often archival trails to follow. Hansard records official speeches. In the case of Treasurer Fadden, rumours that he was once, as Treasurer, too affected by alcohol to complete a speech remain unproven. The official record, Hansard, shows no such speech unfinished. Were such rumours true or simply malicious? — we are left to speculate. Likewise, his deliberations and prompting of Menzies to ban the Communist Party remain only third person accounts — because as yet I have not interviewed anyone who can give a definitive account as to what was the feeling at the time. Did Fadden have concerns about individual freedoms? Was his fear of the communists so encompassing — or was it regarded as a shrewd but cynical political strategy to reduce the appeal of the Labor Party? What were Fadden's motivations — politically strategic or borne out of a genuine loathing of the communist doctrine? Why did he even enter politics in the first place? And what about his personal life? Did he miss his family in the loneliness of Canberra? Did that loneliness contribute to his drinking? Or was time away from Townsville and later Brisbane a welcome relief? Are these questions even important for a study largely concerned with Fadden's contribution to the Coalition? And if they are — where are the answers to be found?

Political biography is an established sub-set of political science. The stories of individuals have added and will continue to add to our understanding of political institutions and history. Due to publishing constraints, biographies commissioned today are increasingly about 'known' recent public figures. Yet there is abundant material out there for would-be biographers keen to research other lives who have walked the corridors of power. Each successive biography written enhances our knowledge of power within the Australian context and contributes to our cultural capital. It is timely to remember that 'politics is politicians; there is no way to understand it without understanding them' (Barber cited in Walter 1980: xviii).

ENDNOTES

[1] The term 'triangulation' is used in Social Science research to define different data collection techniques that are employed when examining the same variable. When observing a particular event through different lenses (use of interviews, primary sources and secondary sources, personal papers, diaries for example), the researcher develops a more complete and informed picture (Neuman, 1997:151).

[2] (see http://ccat.sas.upenn.edu/bmcr/1995/95.09.22.html).

[3] The American Heritage Dictionary of the English Language, 4th Edition, Houghton Mifflin Company, 2004.

[4] Academics have tended to view the 'indeterminate s nature of political biography' as problematic (Walter (forthcoming); see also, Pimlott, 1990: 224).

[5] Narratives have essential characteristics which include being 'chronological accounts of characters and selective events occurring over time, with a beginning, a middle and an end. They are retrospective interpretations of sequential events from a certain point of view; They focus on human intention and action – including those of the narrator and others' which result in a reconstruction of the life under study (Spina & Dodge, 2005:145).

[6] John Dollard's work was titled 'Criteria for Life History' and was published in the early 1930s.

[7] Fadden's successor was Jack McEwen who, it is argued, did not want the Treasury portfolio and opted to retain the Trade Ministry.

Recording Non-Labor Politics Through Biography

Judith Brett

In this contribution I shall address three issues: first, what questions do biographers ask of their subjects; second, why the history of non-Labor has been written largely through the prism of political biography; and, third, why have non-Labor people not been as assiduous in writing memoirs and autobiographies.

To date, I have written two essentially long political essays on Sir Robert Menzies and an essay on Sir Paul Hasluck. I am currently thinking about whether to do a biography of John Howard.

I essentially came to political biography from political science, rather than the other way around. And, I would argue, one's intellectual origins are important in this project. It does make a difference from where you come. Biographers from different backgrounds will pose different questions.

The questions I asked when working on Menzies focused on the basis of his popular appeal. This was the start but I moved from there to a biographical essay. It made me self-conscious of the sort of questions that I would ask in a biography and the way in which I would begin to analyse them. It seems to me that a 'political life' is not just a life that happens to be in politics. Rather, it is a life which is, in some sense, *made* by politics, and then captured by the political biographer. So, one of the main questions I would seek to ask is: what is the deep source of political energy for that person. What drives the subject especially as politics is essentially an uncertain business? Writing about Menzies — and if I were to do a biography of Howard — there are key questions concerning their political life I would want to try to understand first. What drove them? What were the circumstances and influences? Why did politics have a big attraction for them? How did politics satisfy their psychological needs and what pleasure did it give them?

A biographer reflecting on these questions gets a better sense of how their subject handled power and the political process: why the person wants it; what they want to do with it; how they use it when they have it and, equally, how they do not use it when they have it; what they hold back from; and how they give it up. The biographical project is speculative because it seems to me that we typically only observe how the person exercises power when you see them with it, or they give it up, or have it snatched from them.

Secondly, the history of non-Labor has been mainly told through political biographies. I want to put forward some reasons why this might have been the case. Some of these are to do with the emphasis on *leadership* in the non-Labor political tradition. Given that the non-Labor parties are heirs to the nineteenth century leadership-based parliamentary parties, there is a certain rationale in telling the non-Labor story by telling the story of the leader — if not through their eyes, then at least centred on them. It makes sense in terms of their history. The political cohesion and policy direction of these parties were very much in the hands of the leadership, so it makes sense that that is the story to tell.

But there is more to it. The conservative side of politics tends to subscribe to the 'great man view of history', with an interest in the way an individual can make a difference and represent their time. Typical of the sort of biographies I am thinking of here is La Nauze (1965) on Alfred Deakin. It is not actually a very good biography at all, but it is a very good piece of political history. If you want to know what was going on in the formation of the nation and in Victorian politics at that time, then that is where you go to read about it. But you do not come away from La Nauze's study with a sense of a shaped political life. It seems to me that Deakin is somebody who is crying out for a new biographer along the lines of David Day's excellent biographies of Curtin (1999) and Chifley (2003).

There are arguably three partial biographies of Deakin. There is La Nauze; there is *The Mystic Life of Alfred Deakin* by Al Gabay (1992) that explores his spiritual life; and there is John Rickard (1996) who has done Deakin's women and his family life. But no-one, including La Nauze, has actually put these accounts together into an imaginatively conceived political life.

One of the reasons why there has been an emphasis on biography to tell the story of non-Labor is because of the weakness and fragmentation of their institutional and organisational records. We know a little of the story of the party's formation and reformation, and this is a really big contrast with Labor's political history where there has been a continuous, nationally organised party since Federation and where we have party people who take some care with the records.

On the non-Labor side of politics there are various electoral leagues but, until the formation of the Liberal party in the middle of the 1940s, these various electoral leagues came and went. They have different organisations with different party names in different states; they have different organisational structures in different states, with various short-lived splinter parties. There is an extremely weak co-ordinating centre. There is nothing much for the United Australia Party that even counts as the records of a party organisation. The strength of that party was in the state-based organisations that sustained it. Much of its political energy was actually exerted in the states. Today it would be difficult to publish a biography of state-based political activists and certainly not of the pre-war period. So maybe we can obtain a window through coalition biographies, where state-based activity and the holding of state powers was considered very important. Maybe, too, if we can think of producing some forms of collective biographies, this might be one way we could conceivably write about that period of history and publish that sort of material now.

The weakness and fragmentation of the various organisations is mirrored in the poor evidence base. Apart from biographies, there is an incredibly thin, fragmented and scattered archival base for writing the organisational history of the non-Labor side. There are personal papers but no organisational papers as there is for Labor. This relates to the different formations of the major parties — when the Liberal Party was formed in the 1940s nobody kept the records of the United Australia Party. Most records would have been kept in the state branches and what survived is a very hit and miss affair, and most of what has survived is in personal papers. One reason why the non-Labor story has been told through the lives of leaders is because of the relatively greater access to their personal papers.

This also accounts for the fact that so many of the political biographies of conservatives — such as that of Deakin — and I think this is also true of the biography of Menzies (Martin 1993; 1999) — are weighed down with levels of political detail. There is nowhere else for political detail to be told if it is not told in these biographies. To some extent the large size of some of these political lives is because of the thinness of Australian political history. They are not just about lives but about ways of telling organisational history or the history of intellectual traditions. This can be seen in Inga Clendinnen's essay (2004) on Allan Martin's biographical output. As she describes it, he started out by suggesting interesting biographical questions, thematic questions, thinking that he will shape a life around these questions in a less conventional and more probing way. But he ended up in his studies both of Parkes (1980) and Menzies (1993; 1999) writing very standard, chronological, huge biographies weighed down with political detail.

These biographers are not just writing a biography but piecing together the political record. Without biographies these long periods of political experience would never be written. But it makes these biographies tome-like works because they are more of a vehicle for the telling of political history. The political biography of a conservative is arguably compromised by the need to write the non-Labor history of Australia.

Finally, there is the question of why is it that the Liberals or non-Labor politicians do not write about their own political lives? Why are there fewer autobiographies or memoirs of non-Labor political figures? Do they not view their experiences as remarkable or interesting? Are Coalition leaders less inspiring to the biographical imagination? One would not presume so, but we have been hardly trampled in the rush to publish non-Labor autobiographies.

Occasionally some conservative politicians have gone into print. Deakin (1944) and Hasluck (1977; 1980; 1997), both of whom can be counted as being on the non-Labor side, are our intellectuals in politics and have written reflectively or produced material to some extent. There are also memoirs by people like Percy Spender (1969; 1972) and Howard Beale (1977). But not much has come out in more recent years.

I have thought about these issues for quite some time. And I wonder whether it is related to their philosophical experiences and attitudes to time/history. Liberals believe their party is a party of material progress; it is the heir to the optimism of the nineteenth century political experience in the colonies. Their beliefs reflect the building of a new land, the hardships and hard culture that people endured. Conservatives consider they have built prosperity and added societal materialism to the nation building project. They look more to the future while the past is just not of interest. The lack of memoirs or autobiographies of conservative politicians may be a function of the emptiness of a historical imagination — an inevitable consequence it seems to me of that colonial nation building project.

In my own research I noticed time and again when I was reading through the personal papers of various politicians, how often the phrase, 'the past is behind us, we must look to the future,' comes up in Liberal Party documents. Deakin used the phrase. Malcolm Fraser used it in his day. Alexander Downer used almost exactly the same phrase at the beginning of his ill-fated leadership in 1994. There is no sense of nurturing the past. The past is to be left to rest, not celebrated. This may be due to the party's fractured and turbulent experiences. The party's history during the previous century is but a series of new beginnings and rebirths. It makes sense that they do not want to dwell on their failures and, apart from Menzies, there are no heroes for them.

The 'Life Myth', 'Short Lives' and Dealing with Live Subjects in Political Biography

James Walter

Myths, Training and the Biographer's Approach

Initially, I would like to discuss three points. The first is the problem of dealing with a live subject and the question I pose here is 'who owns *the life*?' This is a question that also applies to dead subjects but it is of particular importance with living subjects. We should be aware of the fact that there are different stakeholders in any life or life story — at least three significant types of stakeholders. The second point I want to address briefly is the training of political biographers, and the third is to mount an argument for 'short lives' — less weight and more insight in biographies.

The question 'who owns *the life*?' seems self-evident initially. It does not really strike you until you start trying to unravel the story, but the difficulty with any biography, particularly of a prominent politician is the need to reconcile the subject's own investment in their 'life myth'. People who are somehow engaged in power and power relations to effect forms of social change are of course concerned with their image, they are concerned with posterity and they are concerned with public perceptions. Those are a set of concerns the biographer has to accept and be aware of. These 'life myth' concerns are also linked to the concerns of their family because you will find if your subject is within living memory or recently dead that the family, too, has an investment and there are certain things that the family do not want to tell. But then there are other stakeholders, including the 'followers', party members, political colleagues, members of cabinets (if they were cabinet ministers or a prime minister). Each of these have a particular version of *the life* that they would want to see supported. And, finally, I think the reason why many scholars start biographies is because we are also stakeholders. The subject of the biography may have had an impact on us and we may feel, as a consequence, that we have some right to explore or understand what made them do what they did, why they succeeded or why they failed. I started writing about Whitlam because, like many of the 'baby boomer' generation, he represented to me the great hope of change, and after his election I had gone overseas, thinking the country was in good hands, only to come back and think, 'what happened?', 'why did it go wrong?' So, that is an example of a different set of stakeholder interests.

Importantly, we need to recognise that those different interests are not going to coincide. They each have a different motive behind them, they lead to different clashes and different sorts of issues arise. Once you start writing the book, you become aware of these sorts of things and you are challenged to balance up these interests. You know the family has told you something, you know the political followers have told you something else. As a writer talking to a general audience, you will have different issues you are trying to unravel, to tell your story. These issues are particular to biography because you can never get inside someone else's head. Hence, it always has to be a inductive process. It is not something where you can say: 'I've got all the facts, so here it is'. In terms of political biography, those sorts of stakeholder issues — and I have mentioned three levels but you could probably think of others — are important because they connect the politics with the person. We are after all looking at these people because they had a public impact of some sort. They have exercised power or suffered from power, or driven policy.

The second thing I wanted to talk about is the issue of training, which is one of the most curious aspects about biography. I have had this curious career where I ended up writing a lot of critique of biography and then, every time I wrote an essay, I seemed to be asked by someone else to write another life. And so I developed a whole back catalogue of material on biography, biographical methodology and so on. Then, a couple of years ago, I was asked by the British Academy of Humanities to contribute an essay on the way biographers wrote about biography — and I had great fun doing it, but the main thing is that most biographers, up until recent times, write about biography only after they have written a biography. None of us was trained to be a biographer. In the course of writing a biography you become aware of the issues and, often at the end of the process, you then write a sort of anguished methodological essay about the problems. Then, of course, the next generation of biographers take absolutely no notice and they do the same thing over again. And when you actually look at these essays, they are all saying things that Lytton Strachey said in 1915. If you look at the preface to his *Eminent Victorians*, virtually all the methodological issues are raised there. I was struck again by this issue when I read Paul Strangio's really interesting article about the problems of writing biography after his biography on Jim Cairns, *Keeper of the Faith* (2002) came out, and I then mapped it against these earlier essays.

We have this curious process where we do not train people to do biography. As Skidelsky, the great Keynes biographer, said, political biography is not something that has been seen as really quite kosher. I was forever getting people coming to me from History departments and Asian Studies departments asking me to supervise their MA or their PhD on biography because their department would not let them do it. I kept saying I know nothing about New Guinea or Indonesia or wherever but I nevertheless ended up supervising biographies in a range of fields that I knew nothing about simply because the students wanted to work on biography and they knew I was interested but their department could not see it as a proper enterprise. We do need to start thinking about trying to train people if they are going to engage in biographical work in a way that we would with any other history or politics project.

The third point I want to discuss is what is the key question we want to answer about a particular figure when we write these 'short lives'. Increasingly I have taken up biographical essays in the context of other books. For instance, in my book on political advisers a long time ago, I used biographical essays in each chapter, as illustrative devices, which tell us about institutional change in an historical context and often they tell us exactly what we need to know. We should not write a biography of someone simply because they are *there*, say, they were a prime minister or were some sort of political figure. I think unless there is an interesting question to be answered, then pass through to the wicket-keeper. Political biography surely has to be about answering some sort of question about how politics works, how institutions work, how policy is made and focussing the inquiry on those sorts of questions by writing preferably 'short lives'. And I think they also bring out the methodological issues very fast because you are challenged from the start to say: what is important about telling your story, rather than simply saying it was a calm and stormy night, mum gave birth in the middle of a storm … People said this man is marked for greatness … So my plea is for 'short lives' and some introspection.

The Problems with Live Subjects

There is much we could say about dealing with live subjects in political biography. Most of the work I have done has been based on elite interviews — in-depth interviews with people who work with key figures. The book on Whitlam started off as a study of the post-war prime ministership. But I never got any further with *that* project. As a political scientist, I have been driven by questions about institutions and how they operate, but in the case of Whitlam, they led to broader questions about how he got to the prime ministership, how he crafted his rise to power. I think Whitlam, with Menzies, is probably the most brilliant Opposition leader that we have seen in Australia. Both rebuilt parties in a way that no other political leader in the post-war period has matched. So the question then became: if Menzies could effectively build the Liberal Party after the disasters of 1941, then come back into power and play a key role in entrenching the party in government and himself as prime minister for another 16 years, what of Whitlam? As party leader, Whitlam was absolutely astonishing in rebuilding the Labor Party in the 1960s but then we have his three years as prime minister.

I never meant my book to say his government was a disaster. In fact it was a very exciting time, and a lot of the things it did were truly ground-breaking.

Rather, my question then was: why did it all go so badly? Part of the answer was because of history: the context changed, they had an agenda for a world that had shifted beneath their feet. So, his problems were not all associated with mismanagement and failure. Yet there was a very substantial amount of mismanagement and failure by him as leader — especially in the end — to accommodate himself with the people he worked with and to economic changes.

So my book was a critical book, and I want to reflect on what happens when you write about 'loaded figures' and you venture into criticism. This relates back to the earlier point about who *the life* belongs to. It was always my view that the stakeholders I was writing for were not the party, and certainly not the leader and acolytes, or the families for that matter. I was writing for the rest of us who may have voted for them, or engaged with them, or possibly even opposed them — but whose lives had been in some way affected. I did not set out to give them the portrait they wanted, but to persuade them of why things turned out as they did, why things happened in the way they happened.

There are three aspects to this: access and intellectual stance; reception of the study; and how you are interpreted later. The first aspect is negotiating access and wrestling with the issue of your intellectual relationship with the party or movement and the philosophy from which you are approaching the study. Writing about Labor figures you quickly come face to face with the tribalism inside the party. The more I got into the research, I was conscious that some people who had reservations about talking to me only talked to me because somebody else said, 'No, that's OK. Jim was a branch member in Melbourne. He's been active in the Labor party. He's one of us.'

Now I do not think you have to be of the same political persuasion to write a good biography about a political figure. There have been some terrific political biographies in Australia by authors not of the same persuasion. Take, for instance, Warren Osmond's biography of Eggleston (1985). When he started writing about a key new liberal figure of the end of the First World War period he had himself been a fairly active member of the radical left at Monash University. In the course of his, unfortunately, all-too-brief life, Osmond moved quite a long way across the spectrum but he started out from this radical position yet wrote a terrifically sympathetic and empathetic intellectual history of the man. We do not have enough intellectual biographies.

The point is you do not have to be a Labor person to write about a Labor figure, nor do you have to be a conservative to write sympathetically about people who are Liberals and various sorts of conservatives. But I found from my experience that while my background helped with getting access it created some problems later with Labor's tribalism, in particular, the notion that if you find out things that are less than positive, it somehow should all be kept in the family.

The second aspect concerns the reception of the study when you are critical. When my book about Whitlam came out, it was immediately tagged as a dreadful rightwing book by many Labor people. Someone actually said to me, you have to be from the other side because it is a critical study. This missed the main point of the analysis — what I was trying to explain was the Labor project and how the Labor enterprise failed. The sense of tribalism and partisanship starts to cut across what is the objective purpose which in my case was to investigate what were the strengths and failures of this sort of administration. What effects did it have on us? Where did it succeed? Why did it go wrong?

The third aspect concerns how subsequent readers relate to the book or essay. This comes back again to 'who owns *the life*?'. You cannot prescribe how you will be read as a biographer. I remember a review of the Whitlam book which was never printed but which the reviewer kindly sent to me. The gist of the review's message was this: I had not written about the Whitlam he could recognise. The review ended with these words: 'You didn't give my Whitlam back to me'. The person who wrote this review was himself a writer of good critical biographies of literary figures who effectively wanted a biography that presented the sort of hero he wanted to read about. I had tackled this issue in the last chapter of my book which had been about why do we look for heroes and where does that lead us. So my only response to the reviewer was that my main aim was to interrogate our own responses to these figures, not to reinforce a sort of idealised picture of somebody who failed because he was misunderstood by the Australian people.

Finally, let me conclude by noting a few problems associated with authorised biographies. Years ago I was introduced to a committee fishing around trying to get what they considered to be a good life of Doc Evatt. In a sense it was not an authorised life because the family were not commissioning it, but it was driven by people who thought we ought to have a good Labor biography of Evatt. The trouble with this approach is that it comes at the detriment of biography. There are so many people busy behind the scenes with a particular version of the hero 'they want to be given back to them', that they set up something that is bound to fail. In this case the failure was the biography of Evatt by Ken Buckley *et al* (1994) which was the result of a committee trying to get the right life of Evatt. The pen-portrait of Evatt by Paul Hasluck may be only 3,500 words but it is much more perceptive than the Buckley *et al* biography. So, too, is the Peter Crockett biography of Evatt (1993) which tells me much more about Evatt than his 'official life' authorised version.

This may be why we will never see a good biography of Whitlam. In a similar scenario played out some years ago, Richard Hall was going to write the authorised biography. Unfortunately Richard died before he completed his work, but his starting point when he took on the job was to write demolition jobs on everybody who had previously written about Whitlam. Such efforts from the authorised biographer seem to fall into the category of advocacy biographies — passionate, partisan and engaged in reconstructing the hero. That is the difficulty with authorised biography as a genre. In many ways it makes the biographical project more, not less, difficult and comes back to that fundamental question about 'who owns *the life*'.

Public Lives, Private Lives: the Fundamental Dilemma in Political Biography

Nicholas Brown

The public life-private life division preoccupies Australian political biography — perhaps not peculiarly so, but certainly in distinctive terms. A consideration of the future of political biography might usefully begin by exploring this division, and asking not so much 'which side of the argument is right?' but seeking to identify what is invested in the issue, and how it reflects the uses to which we seek to put political biography. Such a consideration might tap directly into challenging the ways we construct ideas, policies, problems and solutions by imagining alternative approaches, particularly with reference to themes such leadership, representation and power.

As Tim Rowse noted, reflecting on the many ways in which it is easy for a biographer to disappoint, the reception of his *Nugget Coombs: A reforming life* (2002), and his concentration on the 'public' Coombs, prompted an almost iconic despair from Allan Patience. 'It is almost as if Australian maleness encompasses a seeming soullessness,' Patience despaired, 'or that it possesses an unknowable and perhaps stony heart, like the continent itself.' Where was the 'private' Coombs, or at least a sense of what motivated him, explained his values and accounted for the intersection between his career and other facets of his life? On the other side of the argument — and dealing specifically with political biography — James Walter (2002) has emphasised the necessarily public focus of the genre, dealing as it must with 'how people affect institutions and institutional change'. Further, Walter argued that because of the direct impact of the political sphere on our lives 'we want to understand not only leaders but types of leaders'. 'Political biography', he asserted, 'with its general aims of elucidating leadership, philosophy or institutions, has purposes beyond the individual life'. There is, then, an almost didactic, categorical imperative to a concentration on the public dimension of political lives, particularly given a recent emphasis on exploring the public rhetoric of 'social narratives' that are taken as so central to political influence. Walter concluded these comments, in an essay on Paul Hasluck as 'citizen biographer', by endorsing Judith Brett's view in her study of Menzies that 'the public man is the real man and the task is to read his character where we find it — in public life'.

I am not sure whether, in offering this assessment in *Robert Menzies' Forgotten People*, Brett (1992) was recommending a general theorem or accounting for specific characteristics of her man in his context: the most subtle of her chapters in *Australian Liberals and the Moral Middle Class* (2003) deals with a fusion of public and private around the concept of 'sound finance' and the figure of Joseph Lyons — a study which deals not so much a discrete domain of public rhetoric but with intersecting social networks, 'citizens' movements' and discursive shifts in economics and moral injunction. But, either way, we have a polarity: bluntly, on the one hand, a persistent disappointment at the failure of Australian biography to push beyond the public surface of the subject; on the other, an injunction that it is primarily the public domain of the subject that is the essential concern of the political biographer. What should we do with these contending approaches?

In these brief comments, I want to begin by surveying currents of debate in reviews of political biographies, seeking to develop a general sense of use and expectation surrounding the genre without getting caught up in cursory assessments of individual intention and performance. This quick scan confirms a fairly evenly-balanced division between reviewers who regret pages wasted on years outside political office, and those who judge that the breathless details of career obscured an understanding of the subject. No critic was more scarifying on this issue than Rodney Cavalier (2001), reviewing David Day's *John Curtin: A life* (2000). Cavalier alleged Day paid no attention to the vital issues of factional and political management that Curtin confronted: pages that should have been devoted to the enormity of those challenges, Cavalier objected, were given instead to 'neuritis and Christmas'. Day, for his part, has advocated moving beyond the 'traditional, top-heavy, political biography' to understand emotional and psychological issues, and more fundamentally private issues of shame, guilt and dependency. Cavalier was not convinced. Day's 'end product', he judged, was *not* a political biography. Rather, the 'facile attention to the social and political forces driving both sides of politics', Cavalier swiped, 'is more akin to writing words for balloons in a comic strip, pictures not supplied'.

It can, then, get nasty. And it can also seem that political biography, in such a debate, is allocated the fairly meagre role of confirming a public record (a role perhaps like that noted of recent literary biographies, where — presumably under commercial pressure — a detailed intellectual engagement with the subject gives way simply to a chronicle of works and personalities). What is at stake in these disputes? Two things: a continuing interrogation of the political domain itself – one that might be attuned to how this sphere is created, and changes in its dynamism, rather than being taken-as-a-given; and an opportunity to assess the concepts of public and private as they, too, are products of social and political change, with a fair degree of traffic between them. As Kay Ferres has observed, seeking especially to incorporate concepts of gender into the customary domains of biography, the genre itself 'can be a catalyst of dispute and disagreement about the public interest [what defines it, and is encompassed by it] as well as a document of public lives and careers'. What questions/opportunities might Australian political biography, and the political scientists who use it, be missing in this categorical preoccupation with the public-private divide?

'Political lives', a recent British academic reviewer regretted, were becoming an over-worked genre, reflecting 'a fetish for the ins-and-outs of the political class and moving away from interests in the events and ideas that have shaped modern society'. In contrast, Troy Bramson (2003), reviewing one of the two biographical studies of Bob Carr that emerged in early 2003, greeted the West and Morris book (2003) as 'a welcome addition to the burgeoning field of Australian political biography'. This growing field was defined — in part by its subjects, such as Carr — less by ideology or commitment and more by the mechanisms of leadership, ambition and personality (Bramson savoured Carr's admission that 'to be a good leader you must occasionally be a good butcher'). This sense of politics seems to provide the space in which Australian political biography — as a concept, an exercise and a commodity — flourishes, almost despite itself. Allan Patience, this time welcoming Jenny Hocking's study of Lionel Murphy (1997) (explicitly sub-titled 'a political biography', without really explaining why) as warranting immediate placement 'in the vanguard of Australian political biography', prefaced his review by defining the context for such studies thus: 'Australian politics is best understood in terms of meretricious populism. Its factional elites and cliques publicly parade their pretensions to egalitarianism while behind the scenes they mostly practice a mindless adversarialism, boyo-cronyism and payback politics'. With this as an assumption about what defines the political — and with the inevitable dialectics and explanatory resources it establishes (outsiders/insiders, numbers men, levellers, etc.) — we might begin to wonder whether the end product of Australian political biography is in danger being predetermined by the political processes it purports to describe.

One question we might consider, then, is whether such an interdependence between characterisations of Australian politics and the biographical interest in Australian politicians is altogether healthy. A quick reply might be: 'well, that's how Australian politics is: accept it'. A reviewer of Margaret Simons' essay on Mark Latham in May 2004 suggested that Latham might be 'thanked for the rebirth of the political biography' in Australia — the individual trajectory of a Westie becoming a Whitlam protégé and embodying the new values, morality and experience of aspirational Australia. For a moment, Latham peculiarly embodied/celebrated/created a powerful nexus of biography (public and private) and politics. Yet look what had happened to him by October, as an election run on hasty, superficial policies, uncontested assertions and the 'leadership-as-trust' refrain claimed him completely as its victim.

But is it as simple as that? Might other lessons be drawn from the ways leaders inhabit what they call 'public life' — in itself a very revealing formulation, one which might be contrasted to an older concept of 'public office' in its coupling of a personalized ethical pledge to live the duties of high office through an assumed continuum between leader and people, yet which in turn allows an often very convenient departure from the conventions of a leader's responsibility for the arcane, messy, complex and hidden processes of government, of office ('I was not told …', 'I did not know …'). How might we define the public domain of leadership in the wake of the Hutton Inquiry in Britain[1] or *A Certain Maritime Incident*[2] in Australia? As Richard Sennett has already suggested, the 'public', perhaps especially as it is defined by and around politicians, is not as unchanging, self-evident or straight-forward as we like to think: the first call for a biographer might be to ensure that they explore the kind of historical nuances shaping how that sphere is constructed in context.

So long as each side of political biography (the space and game of politics on the one hand and the identification of the biographical subject on the other) remain so mutually reinforcing and justifying, there is unlikely to be much reconsideration of either. So long as the questions asked of one are pretty much the same as the questions asked of the other, we have a stasis, if not a stalemate. Archetypes, as Neal Blewett has observed — from a vantage both inside and outside the domain of politics — are perhaps predestined to dominate political biography and even autobiography, at the expense of 'private selves' and all that they might represent.

How might we move on this situation? First, perhaps, by closely scrutinising the assumptions we work with. Graham Little (1988) noted that the 'rage for strong leadership' during the 1980s — he was referring to Thatcher, Reagan and Fraser in particular — reflected the distinct role of such politicians as 'moral guides through the uncertainties of the age'. These figures represented a politics that, Little suggested, took on 'what the rest of us have given up on, or are making a mess of' (Little 1988). In that context, in a political culture overshadowed by the strained boundaries of expectations and rights from the 1970s but not yet enmeshed in the ambiguities of globalisation and reconstruction of the 1990s, the prejudices of such leaders were their strengths, and the control they exercised on political agendas remedied the alienation experienced among those who supported them. But are we in the same place now? What kinds of questions might we now bring to assessments of the link between the 'public' of the politician and the 'private' of those who look to them for leadership — the experience of 'middle Australia' as surveyed by Michael Pusey (2003), for example? Laments at the failure of contemporary political leadership — its careerism, evasions of responsibility and populism — are widespread. But to what extent do such characterisations of politics and leadership need accommodate changes in political agendas (post materialism, the politics of identity rather than identity politics, issues that no longer fit with ideological continuums, and so on) or the more fundamental ways in which, so Wendy Brown (1995) argued, a universalised liberal entitlement project has produced its own inherent contradictions in individualised normative identity? It is exactly in asking such questions that political biography might serve as a catalyst in rethinking what we mean by public and private in the first place.

Interestingly, in the remarks quoted above, Neal Blewett went on to suggest the need not necessarily for more intimate, private reflections by/on politicians but for 'grander public myths' that might anchor political lives in meaning. Seen from this perspective, perhaps the public-private distinction is not itself especially useful: the point is more about the kinds of questions we seek to answer through it. It is significant that one of the most consistently favourably reviewed recent Australian political biographies is Paul Strangio's study of Jim Cairns, *Keeper of the Faith* (2002): that aspects of that book most often praised centre on Strangio's success in balancing, with both complexity and dignity, Cairns' political failure and his intellectual integrity. It is not that we are being asked to see a private Cairns behind the public face, but that, in powerful ways, the book prompts an exploration of the evolution of identity in shifting political, personal and social contexts that make such divisions seem superfluous. Similarly, part of the success of Marilyn Lake's study of Faith Bandler has been identified in the subtlety with which Lake registered the costs to Bandler's persona and power amid the transition from 'the politics of persuasion' to 'the politics of representation'; and from discourses of equal rights to those of land rights (2002).

This leads to my second point. What has been recently described as 'the biographical turn' in the social sciences offers a perspective on these issues through an increasing interest in questions of: reflexivity, individualisation and agency that reflect both structural and humanist levels of analysis; and, the construction rather than deconstruction of subjects, premised on understanding specific, enabling contexts of action and amounting to more than the realization of identities or pathologies in identities and psychologies. The concept of reflexivity registers the inherently social nature of the self: its basis in exchange; its embodiment in gesture and disposition. Stuart Macintyre noticed these features well in his study of Syme, Deakin and Higinbotham, demonstrating how their political alignments were in many ways reinforced by patterns of sociability, comportment, manners — what might be termed their *habitus*: an embodied, enacted and mutual subjectivity (1991). Judith Allen achieved something similar in her study of Rose Scott (1994). It is significant that a biographical approach figures so prominently in recent studies of women in Australian politics, and perhaps especially of 'conservative' women (Michael McKernan's *Beryl Beaurepaire* (1999); Margaret Fitzherbert's *Liberal Women* (2004), directly testing and challenging the public/private divide as it figures in the lives of those who, experientially or philosophically, might be most assumed to be its subjects. Such codes of sociability are perhaps easier to decipher in Victorian and Edwardian contexts, and among multiple subjects, and away from the relentlessly masculinised domain of top political leadership. But we need such an approach — a full contextualisation of political manners and agency — if we are to understand the current domain of politics and of politicians, and to make sense of how we got here.

My third and final point might seem like advertising, but is about something more. The *Australian Dictionary of Biography* is preparing to release the august *ADB* as a fully-searchable, integrated website. It is easy to get distracted on websites, as evident in an attempt to define the political sphere through the still incomplete, experimental test-site of the *ADB Online*: a search by politician gives us 1611 matches to individual entries; politics gives us 1233; political gives 1910; public servant gives us 1482. Of the 50 links to the use of the word 'frustration', 9 are to politicians; of the 161 to 'compromise', 68 are to politicians; of the 275 to 'ambition', 52 are to 'politicians'; 7 of the 33 (20%) examples of 'envy' are to politicians, as opposed to 9 of the 94 (or 10%) to 'compassion' and 16 of the 142 to 'wisdom'. A large majority of the mentions of 'oratory' are to politicians — what will be the skill that dominates as we move into the more contemporary period? Of the 556 mentions of 'radical', politicians figure as a large minority among a diverse mix, but they account for the clear majority of 'conservative'. And so on.

But beyond this random sample, I want to suggest a more important point. A resource like the *ADB Online*, as it evolves, is not just a technical tool to do what we do any way but more efficiently; it has the capacity to shape and enable new research agendas, and even to be an agent in recasting questions that are appropriate to the changing interests and questions we will bring to biography. In its first release, later this year, for example, a search on Edmund Barton will take you to the *ADB* entry itself, then on to linked resources (guides to relevant papers, collections, sources), one such link being to the digitised Barton papers at the National Library of Australia, including items ranging from correspondence, diaries and photographs through to newspaper cuttings and menus. As the capacity of the *ADB Online* develops through to links to other collecting institutions — such as Screen Sound Australia, the National Museum — imagine what might be done to 'embody' the lives of political figures, not just as individuals but as figures who can be contextualised in their networks, their opportunities, their experiences, their gestures, memberships, friendships, even their geographies and mobility. But, as I said, this is not just a technical resource. The information age, as Manuel Castells noted (for good or ill), is one in which 'people produce forms of sociability rather than follow modes of behaviour'. So the information age, and the new modes of biography it will encourage/require us to produce, might allow us to explore the history of such forms of sociability — again, refiguring our sense of the relation between the political, the public and the private. Rather than coming to biography — as the iconic big, fat book — to confirm the public record, we might find that we use biography to ask rather different questions of what constitutes a sense of the public in the first place.

ENDNOTES

[1] The Hutton Inquiry was a British judicial inquiry chaired by Lord Hutton, appointed by the United Kingdom Labour government to investigate the death of a government weapons expert, Dr David Kelly. The inquiry opened in August 2003 and reported on January 28, 2004. Its terms of reference were to "urgently [...] conduct an investigation into the circumstances surrounding the death of Dr. Kelly". (From Wikipedia, http://en.wikipedia.org/wiki/Hutton_Inquiry).

[2] Senate Select Committee on a Certain Maritime Incident (2002), Select Committee on a Certain Maritime Incident report, Parliamentary paper (Australia. Parliament) no. 498. The Select Committee addressed, inter alia, the so-called 'children overboard' incident involving the HMAS Adelaide and the vessel known as SIEV 4, and the management of information concerning that incident by the Federal Government and Commonwealth agencies.

Expanding The Repertoire: Theory, Method and Language in Political Biography

R. A. W. Rhodes

Introduction

This essay poses three questions. Why is biography isolated from epistemological debates in political science? Are biographers confined to the archive and the tools of the historian? How do we explain our story? Biographers confront many issues specific to their particular art form (see for example Pimlott 1994, 169-61 and the chapters by Arklay and Bolton in this volume). But they can also confront core issues of theory, method and language central to the enterprise of political science. Yet, whether we look at biography through the spectacles of either mainstream or post-modern political science, both dismiss biography.

As an approach in mainstream political science, biography is criticised because it lacks analytical rigour and does not offer law-like generalisations. For example, Blondel (1969, 5) has consistently argued that both historical and case study methods are limited not only by lack of data but also by their inability to compare and explain systematically the structure and behaviour of governments. The case method is suitable for describing unique events and great men but it does not allow generalisations. It does not 'provide guidelines by which to abstract from reality the "critical" elements which would provide the material for comparisons on a large scale' (Blondel 1981, 67). In a similar vein, James (1992, 254) notes the many ministerial biographies, autobiographies, memoirs and diaries 'are often not much use to a student of Whitehall'. In the jargon of social science, quantitative, middle-range analysis is *nomothetic* analysis — that is, it is systematic and fosters generalisations — whereas biography (or case studies or a historical narrative) is *idiographic* analysis — that is, it is descriptive, focusing on the unique (Riggs 1962, 11).

If we take off our mainstream spectacles and wear those of postmodernism, the critique of biography is even more withering (if that is possible). The contrast between the mainstream political science and the post-modern project is sharp (see Bernstein 1991). The former strives after simplification and successive approximations to a given truth. The latter rejects such truth claims, accepting there are multiple realities and no foundations for asserting the superiority of one interpretation over another. Thus, Rosenau (1992, 118 and 120-21) includes a constructivist and contextualist theory of reality, in which reality is treated as a linguistic convention, among the core beliefs of postmodernism. In other words, 'to the extent that the mind furnishes the categories of understanding, there are no real world objects of study other than those inherent within the mental makeup of persons' (Gergen 1986, 141). Moreover, '[i]f language itself is relative and even arbitrary, and if language is the only reality we know, then reality is, at most, a linguistic habit'. 'There are no independently identifiable, real world referents to which the language of social description is cemented' (Gergen 1986, 143). So, 'all knowledge claims (all facts, truths, and validity) are "intelligible and debatable" only within their context, paradigm, or "interpretive community" (Fish 1989, 141) ... 'Reality is the result of social processes accepted as normal in a specific context'.

Stanley Fish (1991, 13-15) states the dilemma for biographers neatly. He argues there has been a shift from a discourse of the self as a conscious subject endowing the world with meaning to a discourse which explains meaning as the product of *epistemes*, paradigms or structures beyond the grasp of the conscious subject. The self is 'dissolved', so 'the notion of an intentional actor with a history and biography must dissolve too'. Any biography assumes 'notions of agency, personhood, cause and effect' that both govern our readings and are contested and contestable. What price the biography of an intentional actor in this post-modern world (and on this argument in historiography see Jenkins 1995 and citations)?

I want to contest both the mainstream and post-modern characterisations. I defend biographical studies by arguing that an interpretive approach deploying the notions of traditions, beliefs, and dilemmas and using the tools of the historian, the philosopher and the anthropologist can provide analytical narratives and diagnostic generalisations without making truth claims.

I now turn to each of my questions. First, I look at a possible interpretive theoretical approach to biography, focusing on the work of Mark Bevir (1999). Second, I look at methods, focusing on cultural ethnography and using the insights of Clifford Geertz (1973). Third, I examine the role of language and forms of story telling in writing narratives, focusing on Hayden White (1973). I do not claim any of these authors provide the right answer. I do argue these are major issues that biographers can address.

Theory: Beliefs, Traditions, Dilemmas

Interpretative approaches begin from the insight that to understand actions, practices and institutions, we need to grasp the relevant meanings, the beliefs and preferences of the people involved. As John Stuart Mill (1969 [1840], 119-20) remarked:

> By Bentham ... men have been led to ask themselves, in regard to any
> ancient or received opinion, Is it true? And by Coleridge, What is the

meaning of it? The one took his stand outside the received opinion, and surveyed it as an entire stranger to it: the other looked at it from within, and endeavoured to see it with the eyes of a believer in it … Bentham judged a proposition true or false as it accorded or not with the result of his own inquiries … With Coleridge … the very fact that any doctrine had been believed by thoughtful men, and received by whole nations or generations of mankind, was part of the problem to be solved, was one of the phenomena to be accounted for.

Interpretive approaches are typically based on philosophical analyses of meaning in action. Meanings are beliefs and, to explain webs of beliefs, Mark Bevir (1999a) uses the concepts of tradition and dilemma. The concepts of belief, tradition, and dilemma distinguish *interpretivism* from other approaches to political science.

Why Beliefs?

As early as the 1950s, philosophers forcefully criticised positivism but political scientists often fail to take seriously the effects of rejecting a positivist notion of pure experience. Some cling tenaciously to the positivist idea that we can explain human behaviour by objective social facts about people and avoid interpreting beliefs. They try to avoid such interpretation by reducing beliefs to abstract and deductive models or to intervening variables between social facts and actions. However, once we reject the idea of pure experience, we cannot 'read-off' beliefs and desires from objective social facts (Bevir 1999a, 127-173). Instead, we must give prominence to the task of exploring the beliefs and meanings through which people construct their world. Because people do not have pure experiences, their beliefs and desires are inextricably enmeshed with theories. Thus, political scientists have to interpret beliefs as part of webs of beliefs, and locate these webs against the background of traditions and dilemmas.

Why Traditions?

The form of explanation we adopt for beliefs, actions, and practices revolves around the concepts of tradition and dilemma. The idea of a tradition captures the social context in which individuals both exercise their reason and act (Bevir 1999a, 174-220). A tradition is a set of understandings someone receives during socialisation. A certain relationship should exist between beliefs and practices if they are to make up a tradition. First, the relevant beliefs and practices should have passed from person to person and from generation to generation. The changes introduced by successive generations might even result in a tradition's beginning and its present-day formulation having nothing in common apart from the links over time.

Second, traditions should embody appropriate conceptual links. The beliefs and practices that one generation passes on to another should display minimal consistency. Traditions cannot be made up of purely random beliefs and actions that successive individuals happen to have held in common. This idea of tradition differs from that of Burkean political scientists who associate the term with customary, unquestioned ways of behaving or with the entrenched folklore of premodern societies (cf. Oakeshott 1962, 123 and 128-9). At the heart of Bevir's notion of tradition are situated agents using their local reasoning consciously and subconsciously to modify their contingent heritage.

Why Dilemmas?

The form of explanation we adopt for beliefs, actions, and practices revolves around the idea of dilemma as well as that of tradition. A dilemma captures the way in which situated agents are able to bring about changes in beliefs, traditions, and practices (Bevir 1999a, 221-264). A dilemma arises for an individual or group when a new idea stands in opposition to existing beliefs or practices and so forces a reconsideration of the existing beliefs and associated tradition. It is important to recognise that political scientists cannot identify dilemmas straightforwardly with what they take to be allegedly objective pressures within the world. What matters is the subjective or inter-subjective understandings of political actors. Of course, there is often much overlap between the pressures that political scientists believe to be real and the dilemmas that trouble political actors.

Why Narratives?

Our interpretive approach explains actions by reference to the beliefs and desires of actors, and it explains these beliefs by traditions and dilemmas. Political scientists explain many features of political life in this way already (and for several examples see Bevir and Rhodes 2006). Although the relevant beliefs and desires are many, complex, and hard to disentangle, political scientists still turn to them to explain human life. The term 'narrative' refers to this form of explanation; it describes the form theories take in the human sciences (Bevir 1999a, 252-62 and 298-306).

This approach has one major advantage for political biographers; they are off the hook of mainstream criticism. Mainstream political science's preference for a modernist-empiricist epistemology, with its core beliefs of comparison, measurement, law-like generalisation and neutral evidence, no longer provides the relevant yardsticks for judging the value of the political biographer's work. Bevir's interpretive approach with its focus on individual beliefs, actions and practices and use of the narrative form of explanation is consistent with the existing working methods of biographers.[1]

Method

The basic claim made for ethnographic method in general is that '[I]t captures the meaning of everyday human activities' (Hammersley and Atkinson 1983, 2). It encourages the researcher to get out there and see what actors are thinking and doing. It produces descriptive accounts valuable in their own right (Hammersley and Atkinson 1983, 237). It is exploratory and encourages fresh lines of thought. Research strategies and ideas can be adapted quickly. And for those who are so inclined, it can be used to test theory; by, for example, the detailed study of key cases (Hammersley and Atkinson 1983, 24).

For Clifford Geertz (1973, chapter 1), humans live suspended in the webs of significance they have spun. Anthropologists practice ethnology to discover the relevant weaves of meaning. Doing ethnography involves using techniques such as transcribing texts and keeping a diary. More important, it is about 'thick descriptions', about explicating 'our own constructions of other people's constructions of what they and their compatriots are up to'. The everyday phrase is 'seeing things from the other's point of view'. The key point is that ethnographers provide their own interpretation of what the informants believe they are up to, so these accounts are second or even third order interpretations.

Ethnographic description has four characteristics; it is interpretive; it interprets the flow of social discourse; it records that discourse commonly by writing it down; and it is microscopic. It is a 'soft science' that guesses at meanings, assesses the guesses and draws explanatory conclusions from the better guesses. Yet it is still possible for ethnographers to generalise. Theory provides a vocabulary with which to express what symbolic action has to say about itself. Although ethnography rarely aims at prediction, theory still has to 'generate cogent interpretations of realities past' and 'survive realities to come'. The task of the ethnographer is to set down the meanings that particular actions have for social actors and then say what these thick descriptions tells us about the society in which they are found. And this analysis is always incomplete.

An Englishman (in India) who, having been told that the world rested on a platform which rested on the back of an elephant which rested in turn on the back of a turtle, asked ... what did the turtle rest on? Another turtle. And that turtle? 'Ah Sahib, after that it is turtles all the way down'.

The ethnographer will never get to the bottom of anything. Ethnographic anthropology is a science 'marked less by a perfection of consensus than by a refinement of debate' — 'what gets better is the precision with which we vex each other'.

I agree with Fenno (1990, 128) 'that not enough political scientists are presently engaged in observation' and I adapt his stricture to political biography. Biography of living subjects is one opportunity for observation and the tools of ethnography provide the means. To the archival skills of the historian we must now add the participant observation and field notes skills of the anthropologist (on which see Sanjek 1990).[2]

Language

If interpretive theory guides us to and through 'the data', if ethnographic methods provide the tools for collecting data, then White (1973, 1978 and 1987) provides the guide on how to use the data to construct and explain the story. Specifically, he deals with the question of whether the plot and language of our narratives prefigure the explanation. Narratives are the stuff of all the human sciences where narratives are 'as much invented as found' so there is an 'irreducible and inexpungeable element of interpretation' and 'there can be no explanation without a story, so there can be no story without a plot' (White 1978, 51, 82 and 62). Explanation is a multifaceted skill similar to understanding a song; it is about connections, whether between words and music, ideas and institutions, individuals and traditions. It is about comparing webs of interpretation. So, to the question of the correct approach to history, White (1973, 4) answers:

> ... it does not depend upon the nature of the 'data' they used to support their generalisations or the theories they invoked to explain them; it depends rather upon the consistency, coherence and illuminative power of their respective visions of the historical field. This is why they cannot be 'refuted', or their generalisations 'disconfirmed', either by appeal to new data that might be turned up in subsequent research or by elaboration of a new theory interpreting the set of events that comprise their objects of representation and analysis.

White's (1973, chapter 1 and 1978, chapter 2) argues the choice of language or tropes prefigures both the story (and its plot) and, therefore, the explanation. Lacking a shared technical language, politics and history rely on familiar figures of speech (or ordinary language) to create meaning. So, in telling their story, historians give it meaning by the type of story they tell — 'emplotment'. White (1973) identifies four modes of emplotment or archetypal forms of storytelling — romance, tragedy, comedy and satire. We tell our stories by encoding them in one or other of these culturally recognised forms. This emplotment translates the past into a story and in the process explains to the reader what is happening.

Since no given set or sequences of real events is intrinsically tragic, comic, farcical, and so on, but can be constructed as such only by the imposition of the structure of a given story type on the events, it is the choice of story type and its imposition upon the events that endow them with meaning (White 1987, 44).

And in telling our story of an event, an institution, a person we confront the absurdity of the human condition and the importance of human aspiration. As

White (1987, chapter 3) argues, we confront the nihilism of history by constructing shards of meaning from chaos. So, the historian, the biographer, and political scientists should abjure imposing order where there is none and instead focus on the notion of the sublime because human dignity and freedom emerge out of our reaction against the meaninglessness of history; we are transmuted into something higher, nobler, or more excellent.

These remarks are too brief to be described as even an introduction to White's work. They do serve two useful purposes, however. First, they show that all historical works, whether of a person, period or events, are 'constructed'. So, political biographies are often more about the author and his or her constructions than the ostensible subject. Second, White poses the question of the extent to which the choice of literary form predisposes the text to a particular form, of explanation. How we tell a life as a romance, a tragedy or whatever — becomes the explanation of that life.[3]

Conclusion

I have used the work of Bevir on interpretive theory, Geertz on cultural ethnography, and White on the analysis of narratives to provide answers to my questions on epistemology, method and language. There are no conclusions to this short piece because my answers are only illustrations. However, I have tried to make my examples relevant to practitioners of political biography for the same reasons we debate these topics in political science — they broaden our repertoire.

ENDNOTES

[1] For examples see Bevir 2002 on Sydney Webb, and Bevir 1999b on Annie Besant.

[2] For an example of a biography based on participant observation see Watson (2002) on Paul Keating.

[3] For an illustration of this argument compare Campbell's (2001 and 2003) chronological romance of Margaret Thatcher's rise from grocer's daughter to world leader with Seldon's (2004) thematic tale of Blair as tragedy.

John Curtin: Taking his Childhood Seriously

David Day

There are many different approaches to biography and political biography. If I had the skills and training of Judith Brett I may well have tried her psychological approach. But I did not and I was left to fall back on a largely narrative approach. This address is mainly about the writing of *John Curtin: A life* (Day 1999).

I came upon John Curtin very early as a student in Melbourne University when I was doing an essay on the reaction in the Victorian Labor movement to the outbreak of the First World War. I was very struck by Curtin's opposition to the war, right from the beginning, when everybody else (with notable exceptions, such as John Cain senior) was taken up with the jingoism. I experienced a powerful bond of shared experience with Curtin's principled opposition to what he saw as an imperialist war, and his willingness to go to gaol because of conscription.

Later on, writing books on the Second World War, I came across a different Curtin — a Curtin then *introducing* conscription. I have a personal interest in that because I, like Curtin in the Great War, went to gaol during the Vietnam War. I wanted to pursue this *empathy* with Curtin and I also wanted to try to reconcile the apparent contradictions between his anti-conscriptionist stance in the First World War with his conscriptionist position in the Second World War. As I looked more closely at Curtin's personal history, and in particular at his father, I realised that I needed to take his childhood seriously. Thinking about my own life, if I had to write my own life, I would have to take my own childhood, and family relations, seriously. I was struck by the fairly derisory approach that most people take to childhood. It is something to be rushed through until coming to the serious phases of adulthood and, particularly in political biographies, periods in power.

So I started investigating his father. Lloyd Ross (1983), author of the other big biography of Curtin, had also looked at his father because Curtin had talked about his father being the sergeant of police in Creswick in country Victoria, near Ballarat (Ross 1977). Ross found out that, in fact, Curtin senior was not a sergeant at all by writing to the Commissioner of Police and asking for the record of Curtin's police service. The Commissioner sent back a very brief letter with the bare bones of that service, saying that he had been a constable in Creswick basically. I do not know whether he would have been able to obtain the full service record. The full service record is quite different and shows the burden of shame that Curtin's father took with him to Creswick.

Those of you who have not read *John Curtin: A life* (Day 1999), come with me on a journey down Base Street, Port Melbourne, with Curtin's father on his nightly rounds as a constable, going past Mrs Jolly's Lolly Shop, seeing the shop assistant put up the shutters and following her down the corridor, grasping her to him and fondling her breast and planting a big kiss on her. And then, when she, affronted, calls the proprietress, Curtin senior just goes off on his rounds as if nothing had happened. This was very striking and opened up all sorts of questions as to what was going on here with Curtin's father.

Later on, when he resigned from the police force, with rheumatoid arthritis, so it was believed, there is a whole file in the police records about his medical examination, showing this in order for him to get superannuation. It seemed to confirm the story of the rheumatoid arthritis but, then, I am not sure that Ross ever got the death certificate of Curtin senior. The death certificate tells a different story — that he, in fact, died of syphilis and it was the effects of syphilis apparently that forced him to leave the police force. This was covered up in order for him to get superannuation.

This gave insights into the sort of childhood that Curtin would have had in Creswick. It was not an idyllic country childhood, a rural childhood, at all. He lived with an irascible father, a father who probably suffered from the same sort of bipolar disease as Curtin himself. Once this was understood, it was obvious that the childhood could not be dealt with in a few pages or even in a single chapter. I took several chapters to bring Curtin to age 18.

There was another incident in his childhood as well that I hinted at in the book but was too speculative to give full-blown treatment. But what I tried to do was explore the reasons why Curtin became so strongly committed to politics at so early an age. It seemed that it probably occurred not in the back streets of Brunswick with his deprived childhood so much, but possibly in the vestry of the Catholic Church in Carlton where Curtin was an altar boy. Ironically the Catholic priest who baptised him earlier in Creswick later came to Carlton. It seemed to me from various tantalising glimpses throughout Curtin's life that he may well have been abused as an altar boy in Carlton. This is something that I hinted at but, for fear of being shot down in flames, did not put explicitly into the book. It raises many questions as to what you do put in and what you do not.

I did not allude to this possibility just because child abuse was the flavour of the month — it was in the newspapers at the time. It was also suggested in Curtin's reaction to the church itself and his refusal to admit a priest at the Lodge when he was dying. He never went into a Catholic church or any other church again once he had left the Salvation Army in his teenage years. Even if close friends were marrying, he would not go to the wedding, though he would go to the reception afterwards. The only time he was prevailed upon to go to a church was in Canberra when his close female friend Belle Southwell prevailed upon him to attend the re-dedication of the Presbyterian church and the minister was struck by the way he was shuddering from fear or anxiety when he was prevailed upon to speak during the service. So I was trying to make sense of all these things but there was no way of confirming it.

But it raised many questions about what to put in and what not to put in. I also realised how confronting it is to write a biography — not only for the biographer but also for the family of the person, particularly if there are still living children. Had I been able to meet Curtin's son, he may well have been able to give me some insights into this. But he simply refused to meet, and did not want another biography of his father. He was not only Curtin's son but Curtin's namesake, so he did not want another book about John Curtin because he said he would face ribbing down at the bowling club if there was another book in the bookshop. We had a nice conversation on the telephone, quite a long one, but that was as far as he would allow me to go.

It raised all sorts of questions for me, then, knowing that he was opposed to me even writing a biography, and he was quite sick at the time as well. As to who owns the lives of dead politicians, is it the biographer? In one sense — as a subject — Curtin 'belongs' to David Day, biographer. In another sense, Curtin — or rather, his memory — belongs to his children and grandchildren.

So how sensitive does the biographer have to be to the wishes of the family and, as well, I guess, to the wishes of the political party, and political supporters or even to academic colleagues down the corridor who have fixed ideas as to what constitutes a political biography?

Ministers, Prime Ministers, Mandarins: Politics as a Job

Patrick Weller

I am a political scientist. I seek to ask those political science questions at the core of any appreciation of how the political system works; especially the complexities and the different angles or perspectives. My first training, however, was in history. The combination of the two disciplines means that I have always been primarily interested in the way institutions work, the way power is exercised, the interactions between individuals and the institutions with which they work – institutions they often help shape and which in turn shapes them. I try to understand the capacity of people in a given timeframe and the opportunities provided by the institutions and events that confront them. Consequently I have written primarily about political practices and political processes, about the positions and office-holders in politics, the challenges they face and the frameworks that guide behaviour.

Over time I have written what can almost be called 'collective biographies', studies of ministers, prime ministers or senior officials — sometimes called 'the mandarins'. I have tried to work out how they actually operate, how they conceive of their roles, how they approach problems and what opportunities and perils they see ahead. In the case of the mandarins I used some brief mini-biographies as illustrations of the themes I had identified.

I also wrote two book-length studies of individual actors — Malcolm Fraser, Liberal Prime Minister from 1975-83 and John Button, Labor's Industry Minister from 1983-93 (1999). I am going to refer to both of them, even if neither is political biography in the conventional sense. Let me explain how I got there.

In the early 1980s I read a book by Robert Caro on Lyndon Johnson. Caro has now completed three volumes of this biography and Lyndon Johnson is not yet president. The third volume is a thousand pages. It is, in a sense, a study of the workings of the United States Senate as much as it is a biography of LBJ. What makes these books so good is the sense of place and circumstance: an understanding of Texas politics or Senate procedures that put Johnson in context. They describe not merely the crises of Lyndon Johnson's life but the day-to-day activities and strategies that explain how and why he was so effective. Caro shows how LBJ campaigned for outcomes on a day-to-day basis. Caro goes beyond the fact that Johnson won an election to illustrate how he got the numbers in the Senate when he was majority leader of the Senate. It is those mechanics of power rather than the crises that I actually find so fascinating. It is the routine, the daily grind, politics as 'a day at the office', which underpins great achievements. If Richard Neustadt (1960) talked of the president's power to persuade, Caro showed in devastating detail how one future president did it (Caro 1982, 1989, 2002).

But I could find no Westminster equivalent that could show *how* a prime minister or minister operated. I wanted to know the *hows* and the *whys* of the way that a cabinet operates to understand why the prime minister generally wins, whatever the circumstances are. What is the job of prime minister or minister, how it is translated into a series of meetings and decisions, all day, every day? Routine, not crisis, is the normal mode of ministerial life. Days are structured by meetings, not by seminars to discuss political philosophy. They make decisions, day in, day out, as part of a series of pragmatic, sequential issues that fall or are selectively isolated for their decision. They jump from topic to topic. Life is a mosaic of pieces that provides a pattern only in retrospect. Ask how they approach the job and the response will be that they did what the job required. That is what ministers or prime ministers do; there is choice, but within a context.

So, what I set out to do in the books on Fraser and Button was to ask questions about how these individuals operated, how they achieved what they tried to, what their objectives were. How did they operate within the institutions in which they found themselves in order to seek to shape the outcomes? That approach had some implications. In a sense I was looking at people through a prism of institutions, at people in context. I was interested in them as institutional actors, as prime minister or minister. That raised questions about what I was, or was not, interested in as part of my study. With Fraser, the title is *Malcolm Fraser PM*. That concentration on the office allowed me to limit my inquiries: when I went to see him the first time, he said: 'Well, should the Governor General have done it?' I said: 'Well, you weren't actually Prime Minister at the time so it's not covered in my scope, but since you ask, no'. He said: 'Yes he should have, but earlier'. I certainly have views on the ambush, but my principal concern was how the means of arrival in office affected his incumbency of it.

I took the view in both cases that when the office door closed, I lost interest. Quite consciously I was interested in them as politicians, operating as politicians; as long as it did not directly affect their performance, what they chose to do outside of that was none of my business. That was particularly so as they are both very much still alive and were very much still alive when I was writing. Does this make it less than a full biography? Of course. But as I was interested in people as politicians, I never pretended otherwise. Besides, I think subjects have a right to reasonable privacy. So I consciously said this is a public story. The subtitle to the book on Button is *A Labor life* because it was designed to show how John Button worked within the Labor Party rather than a biography in the sense of from go to whoa (or woe). Not everyone appreciated the limitations I put on myself. But then, as I suggested at the beginning, I am more political scientist than biographer, and my interests were clear.

I used different ways of doing it. For Fraser I was interested in different institutions through which he operated so the book is divided into the arena in which he worked: the Prime Minister's office, the Cabinet, the Parliament, the Party. It examined the segmented sections within which a prime minister operated. But such segmentation is artificial as a prime minister works in all at once. The job is a single role with multiple challenges. I wanted to show what levers were available and where the limitations might be.

For Button, quite deliberately, I tried a more traditional chronological approach, partly just to see if I could do it. It was just an interesting exercise. I had written other sorts of books, so, could I write a book like that and did I like writing such a book? There was partly a personal challenge to find out what I was capable of doing. It was much more chronological and much more concerned with tracing his rise through the Labor Party and explaining how someone who, by all the rules of the Labor Party, should never have got anywhere close to Parliament or power. After all, the Labor Party in Victoria in the 1960s was dominated by the far left and John Button was certainly not of that ilk. Yet he managed to win and retain a position in the Senate without having been a member of any of the major factions. He was leader of the Labor Party in the Senate for nearly 13 years, a remarkable stint, and he was a senior minister for 10 years at the same time. By all the unwritten rules of the Labor Party, he should not have been there at all.

I was trying again to explain the way he charted his way through. As anyone reading the book will know, I was not terribly interested in the details, for instance, of his ten years as Minister for Industry. I was interested in how he learnt to be minister but exactly what his industry policy was, was not part of the story I wanted to tell. It goes back to Jim Walter's question: unless you have some interesting questions, something that drives the story, what are you doing there? And my questions were about the way that he worked on those sorts of exercises.

The nature of the evidence changes, too, if these 'collective biographies' into political leadership are the type you wish to write. There are two reasons. If you actually want to know who wins on a day-to-day basis, you do not find it in the newspapers. You do not find it in most traditional histories. History by nature is more concerned with the big events and the exciting factors than it is with what goes on in a cabinet meeting. It is not concerned with why, day after day, Fraser could win or Button could win and why they achieved what they did. You then start by necessity; you have to use interviews. Second, the documents are not available for much of the time. Although Fraser, quite remarkably, said to me: 'Well, would you like to see my papers and the cabinet documents?' And I said: 'Oh yes, please'. He said: 'Well, I'll check them out. I'll read them first and then decide what you can see'. Then he, I think, realised what was involved and said: 'Oh hell, just see them'. And when I used to interview him, he used to say: 'Go and check the papers. See what they have to say'.

Neither Fraser nor Button asked to see a copy of the manuscript.

Fraser gave me access to the cabinet papers up to 1983 which is better than the 30 year rule imposed under the Archives law. But that is a little unusual. And they were fascinating. I did not get the cabinet notebooks unfortunately. They have not been released yet although at one stage Geoff Yeend did offer to read them to me, but never had the chance to do so. You did at least get an immediacy which you then could cross-check with interviews. Usually there is no such option. For current work you need to rely primarily on the public record.

Interviews are cumulative; you talk to one person, they say such and such happened, and you think, that is interesting. You talk to three people and they are still saying it happens and then you feel perhaps there is something to it. And you talk to 15 people and they all say the same thing or give the same impression; by that stage you reckon you have pretty well got it nailed. Towards the end you have talked to people, not because you expect to find something new but it is a case of adding to the evidence, one story upon another, until you actually are reasonably sure that this is the way the system worked in cabinet or this is the way that Malcolm Fraser operated. Interviews are for routine, an alternative to documentation because it is the routine that tells you how and why people win. For that you have to do it with the living. No-one sits down generally and details these sorts of things in their memoirs, and besides, there are no follow-up questions in memoirs, as there are in interviews. You have to talk to people about how the prime minister did it or how did they usually do it in those circumstances. It is the nature of the evidence about writing, the recent events.

I started both books after the relevant person had left power. It would be very, very difficult, I think, to do it while they are currently in power. A biography of Howard written now would be difficult because the big question is: how did he leave power. A number of people, including me, were asked by *The Age* to rank the top ten prime ministers since the war, to put them from 1 to 12. Unwritten in that exercise was the problem that we do not yet know what happens to Howard in the end. As a result, some people put him further down their rankings. I had him higher up but there was always this sort of unwritten proviso: what happens at the end?

But with all the caveats, interviews do serve very useful purposes. Without them the picture we have would be greyer. I have now got interviews of ministers and mandarins going back to 1978, and I will give them to a library if they want to take them. They provide a bank of changing experience. But we also need to be aware that they, as much as any memoir, are concerned to paint an image of the role of the speaker that by itself should not be taken as given. Check one against another, calculate the bases, appreciate the angles, and they are as useful, and as fallible, as any written record by the same person.

In the end I hope that I presented an account that gave some idea of the challenges that the subjects faced and, at the same time, portrayed the structures within which they worked. They did not re-invent the roles of prime minister or minister; they took them on. They may have shaped the jobs they filled, but there were expectations they had to meet, too, routines they had to follow. Like everyone else they went to work and did their job. We need to understand what that job was because their decisions as incumbents may affect us all.

Biography and the Rehabilitation of the Subject: The Case of John Gorton

Ian Hancock

When I was an undergraduate, some years ago, I read a comment on biography by Sir Lewis Namier, the magisterial historian of eighteenth century British politics. Namier thought that someone embarking on a biography was no better qualified for the task than a woman who applied for the position of minding children and said in support of her application that she herself had once been a child. No doubt with the advancement of so many academic disciplines and the multi-skilling of so many academics, Namier's dismissal of biography is now out of date for most biographers. But not so in my case. When, therefore, I was commissioned to write a biography of Sir John Gorton (2002), a chapter on Sir Robert Askin (2006) and a long entry on Harold Holt in the *Australian Dictionary of Biography* (1996), I realised that my immediate problem was myself. Very simply, my qualifications, let alone my experience, did not equip me for the task.

Yet historians are always writing about events, people and context removed from their area of familiarity. So it did not really matter that, unlike Gorton and Askin, I was born of parents married to each other, or that, unlike the private schools Gorton and Holt attended in Victoria, mine had begun to curb the excesses of muscular Christianity if not of gender isolation. It did not matter that, unlike Holt's father, mine did not sabotage my self-esteem by seducing and then marrying the girlfriend I brought home to meet him. I did feel, however, that my stint as a staff sergeant in the school cadets, and firing a First World War rifle on field days, together with a general lack of intestinal fortitude, did not really prepare me to write about John Gorton. After all, he was a wartime fighter pilot, who barely survived two horrendous crash landings, whose ship was torpedoed after leaving Singapore, and who spent days on a raft waiting for a Japanese submarine to finish him off.

Nor did my time as the Communist Party Prime Minister of my school's Parliamentary Society actually assist my understanding of the political process. Even then, I suppose I did learn something about branch stacking, having used fellow boarders to get myself elected, and I also learnt, when later observing the federal Parliament, that juvenile behaviour can continue beyond adolescence. Moreover, my brief stints as a Liberal Party branch member, which always ended when I could invent a point of principle upon which to resign — that is, to escape — did at least alert us to the tedium and triviality and occasional manic absurdities of grass roots Liberal politics.

Despite my doubts, I decided that after all those years of studying political history in Africa and Australia, and observing and sometimes dining at what Manning Clark called the 'Banquet of Life', I could give it a go. So, despite decades of theoretical under-nourishment, and feeling quite healthy nonetheless, I sallied forth remembering the tale of Hilaire Belloc's water beetle — best just to swim, for to stop and think, would be to sink.

That said, in writing the biography of John Gorton, Prime Minister of Australia between 1968 and 1971, I was troubled by two serious problems. First, I was officially a member of Gorton's staff. And, unlike many other biographers, I did not choose to write about my subject. In my case the subject chose me. I was paid a salary and expenses (which rewarded me well above the average royalty returns). Clearly, I risked being dismissed as a mere hireling employed to write a hagiography. Interestingly, no reviewers condemned me on that account, though some thought I could have been more critical.

James Walter has already flagged what became my second problem, though I do not much care for the term 'stakeholder', if only because universities have been demeaned and self-demeaned for too long by such usage. I had a research assistant — a particular research assistant whose name will be familiar to many — Ainsley Gotto. She was Gorton's one-time principal private secretary or chief of staff, who was appointed when she was just 22 years of age. She was also, for the purposes of the Department of Finance, my supervisor. In addition, she kept a watching brief on Gorton's behalf and, in the process of what diplomats would call a free and frank exchange, but I like to think of as a sparkling friendship, I learnt much about why Gorton chose her to administer his office and why and how she caused him considerable grief. The important point is that Ainsley probably wanted, and the second Lady Gorton most certainly wanted, was not so much a biography as rehabilitation.

Although I started out thinking that Gorton was not even a good prime minister, I came to agree that rehabilitation was more than justified. The unelected and unelectable members of the fourth estate, who had dismissed him as 'Bungles' and 'Jolly John,' had successfully cemented a number of conventional wisdoms which do not survive even a cursory examination of the voluminous official and personal records at the time, let alone a host of interviews. Yes, he did, on his own admission, drink too much. Yes, he broke what we Anglicans would think of as the Seventh Commandment (and he did so while he was prime minister). But was he lazy and none too bright? The marginal comments on Cabinet submissions alone should dispel both pieces of nonsense. He had more time on his hands than Harold Holt because of his instant grasp of the heart of any matter. And he was certainly sharper than Billy McMahon who underlined pretty well everything just in case he missed something important. For a bloke who claimed he majored in rowing whilst at Oxford, but put together a top upper-second when he could spare the time, John Gorton was probably one of the brightest minds ever to inhabit the Lodge.

Rehabilitation was no problem in another respect. The experts told me that Gorton was the best Navy Minister of the twenty-one Australia has so far had, the only rider being that the competition was not exactly fierce. More importantly, it was Gorton, initially under Menzies and then on his own, who piloted the Commonwealth's entry into primary and secondary education (to the enormous advantage of poorer Catholic schools), and who promoted the growth of the colleges of advanced education. As Prime Minister, Gough Whitlam sent a private note to Gorton — 'I intend to finish some of the things you started'.

The problem I faced was this. While I was happy to restore the public face and, indeed, to show it in what that great sage Mungo McCallum called 'tedious detail', I wanted to explain something which began to bother me when I finished telling the story. Why did this man *not* become an outstanding prime minister? He was, after all, more talented than most of our political leaders, and had a gift for touching what are sometimes called 'ordinary Australians', surpassed only by Bob Hawke in modern times. Some of the answers to my question could be found in the Menzies-led Liberal Party of the 1950s and 1960s. But I soon realised that important answers lay within Gorton himself. I was then reminded of Namier's dismissive remark. I was suddenly alone, naked and without qualifications.

Whether his illegitimacy played upon his mind (as some who do not know him well would have us believe), it probably did not require taking 'Psych 1' to recognise that Gorton's early life, where he was constantly being farmed out and denied affection, taught him to fend for himself, to do it his way. He would always be John Gorton, the fighter pilot, alone in the air, who wanted to be, and had to be, his own man. This was the John Gorton, the committed Australian nationalist and centralist who had, I believe, the right idea of taking on States' rights, but who as an outsider within the Liberal Party, never understood the need to coax and to compromise or even knew how to do so. Some of the stakeholders preferred this story, and wanted the story of his personal relationships to be glossed over. The saving grace was always Gorton himself: he could not care less, and told me to get on with it.

It was not just his childhood which moulded the man. Consider his last year at Geelong Grammar. It was 1930, the first full year of the Great Depression. James Darling, the new self-styled Christian socialist headmaster, arranged for the senior boys to deliver food parcels to the homes of the unemployed in Geelong. Decades later, Gorton was still speaking about the impact of seeing people battered by circumstances beyond their control, and of witnessing resentment in the eyes of broken men who had faithfully served their country in the Great War. I believe a line can be drawn between that experience and the Gorton who irritated the conservatives in his own party by thinking that social reform was more important than the forward defence of Australia.

And then there was Gorton's own war. Like so many of his contemporaries, he returned to Australia, in his case with his face disfigured by injuries, determined to transmit the values of war time service to the task of post-war reconstruction. As John Gorton himself put it: they wanted to build on the political freedom won on the battlefield, to make a better and more secure world for all Australians. That freedom, he believed, was threatened by the Chifley Labor government's decision in 1947 to introduce bank nationalisation. So, as a struggling orchardist and shire councillor from northern Victoria, he joined the anti-socialist crusade which bought many ex-servicemen to Canberra in 1949. By chance and without adequate training, he had the opportunity twenty-one years later to address those things which had so moved him in the 1930s and 1940s.

In March 1971 half of his colleagues voted against him in a 'no-confidence' motion in the party room. He gave a casting vote against himself — he did not know the rules, he did not have to, as no-one else did either. The wife of one of his colleagues would later say: 'Australia was ready for John Gorton, but the Liberal Party was not'. Determined, as always, to do it his way, he had not bothered to take his party with him. Excited in 1968 to get the job, he threw it away in 1971 because he was sick of the intriguers his lone hand had helped to foster, and who had become exasperated with his maverick leadership.

I could, as a biographer, rehabilitate him as a reformer and an idealist but, in trying to explain his downfall, I had to probe all of Gorton's complexity — to the annoyance of some of the stakeholders. There were, fortunately, many relieving moments. One of them involved investigating the fist fight which took place in Parliament House during a Senate dinner break. Gorton came to blows with Don Willesee, a Labor Senator from Western Australia. The seven men I interviewed, including the two participants, could not agree on where exactly in the building the incident occurred, when it occurred, why it occurred, or who won. Triangulation was impossible.

Aboriginality and Impersonality: Three Australian Indigenous Administrative Memoirs

Tim Rowse

The Indigenous public servant is a relatively recent phenomenon — a product of the maturing of the programs of assimilation and the inception of the programs of self-determination. That the Indigenous administrative memoir is recent follows from this, but it is also relevant to point out that the genre Indigenous autobiography is itself not yet fifty years old. In this essay, I will tell you about three Indigenous autobiographies in which the authors (all male) have produced an account of themselves partly by reflecting on their times as a public servant. In each case, the theme 'impersonality' is prominent, but each time in a different way.

Charles Perkins

Charles Perkins wrote *A Bastard Like Me* (1975) early in his career as a public servant. Perkins recalled 'as a compromise' his accepting a research officer position in the Office of Aboriginal Affairs in 1968. He would forsake political activism in order to realise 'the possibilities in the position ... I knew that I was, in a way, being bought off', but he welcomed the 'administrative experience' and the opportunity for influence (1975: 109). The first six months in the job he recalled as 'degrading': 'People set out deliberately to show me where I belonged (or should belong), and to make me feel completely an inferior person and nonentity in Aboriginal affairs' (1975: 109).

Before taking up the job, however, Perkins visited many countries in a three month trip abroad. He came to dislike many Australian diplomatic officials. Their duties included helping him, but 'they regarded me as inferior in intelligence' and he inferred that they looked forward to his moving on. 'I came to the conclusion that most diplomats are professional liars, two-faced' and too mindful of their own convenience to be effective servants of the Australian public. 'I feel they live in a world of their own and regard others as bloody intruders' (1975: 122). He found the Washington Embassy officials especially obstructive. One of them, he recalled, accused him of 'jumping on the racial bandwagon' (1975: 126). By the time he and his wife reached Moscow (travelling West to East) Perkins had come to think that 'perhaps my reputation at other Australian Embassies had preceded me and they were fearful that I might embarrass them' (1975: 138). Upon returning to Australia, he reported his displeasure to a debriefing attended by Paul Hasluck and by senior officials of External Affairs. The notes on that meeting are presumably in the National Archives and would make interesting reading.

Perkins commenced work with the Office of Aboriginal Affairs in March 1969. Although his position was junior, he was a figure of great interest (whether positive or negative) to senior political figures, as his book attests with its many brief anecdotes about conversations with people such as Gorton, Anthony, Bryant and Hasluck. It must have been difficult to reconcile the roles of national political figure and junior public servant. I suggest that we understand this specific difficulty as overlaying and exacerbating the trials that induction into the classical traditions of the public service imposes upon any person who is politically opinionated and politically active. Perkins writes — not wholly in criticism — that 'the bureaucracy swallowed me up' (1975: 157). He had to learn what he calls 'paper warfare': writing and responding to writing, and doing both within a large, opaque hierarchical establishment in which he was but one junior functionary.

As well, Perkins found the social environment of his work place cold, unfriendly and abounding in insults to his pride that were no less hurtful for being, often, unintended. 'I had to cover it up by saying nothing and swallowing my pride' (1975: 158). Though he conceded that he had always found it difficult to make friends, he also attributed his social difficulties in Canberra to 'the typical impersonal nature of the public service'. 'Impersonality', he then remarks, is 'one of the tragedies in the public service' (1975: 159). Perkins suggested a way to overcome this systemic disaffection.

It would seem a good thing that public servants work elsewhere every ten years to meet the general pubic on a different level and to humanize them. It would do them personally a lot of good, their families, their work and the general public. Perhaps if superannuation benefits were extended to the public service and the private sector alike, people could move more freely. A lot would move out of the public service and make a great contribution to private industry if this were done (159).

The Department of Aboriginal Affairs could be improved by making it a statutory authority allowed to recruit Aborigines to senior positions, he suggested (1975: 194). 'There are just too many whites in Aboriginal Affairs — unfortunately the good ones leave in disgust or disillusionment or get depressed' (1975: 196).

By the time he penned these thoughts, the Whitlam Government had both raised the possibility of administering Aboriginal affairs in new ways and revealed to Perkins the inflexibility of the public service culture and of the Council for Aboriginal Affairs. As well, the Australian press continued to be, in his view, 'anti-Aboriginal' (1975: 182). Perkins thought that he had failed to live up to the expectations that other Aborigines had of him. Early in the Whitlam

Government, he was promoted from clerk class 7 (third division) to Assistant Secretary (second division [now senior executive service]). He had not internalised the disciplines expected of a public servant. It was while on leave from that position that he wrote in *A Bastard Like Me* of his disappointment that he had been suspended in 1974 for making statements that the Government found embarrassing. 'I knew that I was breaking public service regulations but the issues were too vital and the regulations therefore just had to go' (1975: 196).

Perkins was not only at odds with the regulations about confidentiality of advice, he also thought that the department was hamstrung by its concern for financial administration. It did not allow Aborigines to make such mistakes as 'some mishandling of funds or money seemingly wasted on special projects ... The well-worn myth is that Aborigines are irresponsible with money. This is propaganda to deny Aborigines the right to make their own decisions' (1975: 178). If Aboriginal people make mistakes and 'suffer,' then they will learn to be independent and confident, Perkins argued. (However, he did not concede that in the regime of strict financial administration about which he complained the Department had a way both to define 'mistakes' and to impose 'suffering'.)

Gordon Matthews

When Gordon Matthews, author of *An Australian Son,* joined the Department of Foreign Affairs, he believed that he was of Aboriginal descent. He had been adopted as a baby and did not know who his natural father was. While at school (at Scotch College, Melbourne) he had been subject to racist teasing and, in this cruel way, offered the identities 'Abo' and 'Boong'. While resenting such teasing, he considered it possible that he was of Aboriginal descent. As an undergraduate at the University of Tasmania, he was persuaded by an advocate of Aboriginal education that he probably had 'Aboriginal blood' and that he was entitled to a Commonwealth study grant. He was attracted to this possibility, for the certainty it gave him about his identity, and because he felt that 'I had suffered for my colour' (1996: 76). His adoptive parents and the Commonwealth accepted his decision.

He subsequently found out that his natural father was not Aboriginal but Sri Lankan. Between the act of identification and this discovery, Gordon learnt to be Aboriginal. One lesson came directly from the Australian public service. Gordon applied for a position in Foreign Affairs. In the interview (which took place in the late 1970s or early 1980s), he was told that his Aboriginal background was one of the qualities that made him attractive to the Commonwealth. Once in the job, his contact with other Indigenous public servants gave him the sense that, for the first time in his life, he was 'participating actively in Aboriginal Australia' (1996: 89). As well, he was assigned to duties in the Department's promotion of awareness of Aboriginal culture and in its recruitment of Indigenous staff. The Commonwealth's multi-faceted promotion of Aboriginality was a nurturing context for Gordon, making it unimportant, for a while, that he had never proven to his own satisfaction that his father had been Aboriginal. However, that question never completely left his mind, and he undertook a long search for the identity and whereabouts of his natural parents. Most of the second half of his book is about how he and his natural parents and siblings came to terms with one another, once he presented himself to them.

Among the anxieties provoked in Gordon by his discovery that his father was not Aboriginal was a certain insecurity about his status in the Department of Foreign Affairs. The Bicentennial was looming, and in that politically sensitive context it was likely that Gordon's Aboriginality would become an even more salient part of his work for the Australian government. How could he tell his superiors that he was not, after all, an Aboriginal man? In the event, Gordon's boss took the revelation well and decided that, apart from altering his personal file, the Department need not make his change of ethnic status a public matter. His Indigenous public service colleagues sympathised with the personal ordeal of 'de-Aboriginalisation', and they treated him the same as before. Indeed, 'indigenous officers in the Department insisted I continue to participate in the informal group we had established to discuss issues relevant to indigenous staff' (1996: 210). One 'senior Aboriginal leader' told him that he was still Aboriginal because his life had been shaped by the assumption that he was. As well, as Gordon writes, 'I had experienced first-hand what it felt like to grow up Aboriginal in mainstream Australia' (1996: 211).

To grow up in 'mainstream Australia' in Gordon's times (1960s and 1970s) meant being positioned both negatively in popular culture and positively in official culture. Not only was he taunted with epithets such as 'boong' and 'Abo' at Scotch College, but he was also favoured by state practices of representing 'Aboriginal heritage' as part of Australia's nationhood. And the positive valuation of Aboriginality in official cultural policy, by the 1980s, was generating among Indigenous public servants in Canberra a discourse on Aboriginality in which the facts of genealogy were less important than the social promptings of identity politics.

Wayne King

Wayne King, the author of *Black Hours* (1996) grew up about ten years ahead of Gordon Matthews, in Ipswich and in a working class Aboriginal family tormented by the father's alcohol problems. Upon leaving school, Wayne became a clerk in the Queensland public service. Although he was conscious of the racist unfairness of Queensland society, Wayne was not attracted to political activism. Rather, he sought his escape by taking a job in Canberra as a telex operator in the Department of External Affairs in 1966. In Canberra, he also found it possible to form a homosexual relationship, to be 'camp', in the parlance of the day. In 1967, he and his boyfriend Garry moved to Sydney, and Wayne got a job with

Mitsubishi. His friends in Sydney included activists in Federal Council of Aboriginal and Torres Strait Islanders. As the issues of Aboriginal rights became more prominent in Australian public life, so, too, did the racism of his and Garry's gay acquaintances become apparent. It was difficult to deal with their racism, because Wayne found that there was a difference between the easily assumed liberalism of conversation about Indigenous political issues and the subtle racism that remained so powerful in his social life that he and his Aboriginal friends could not even talk to each other about the shame that they felt in being Aboriginal. By 1970, Wayne had found that no milieu in Australia offered him escape from white racism.

He applied to join the United Nations as a conference typist and moved to New York. There it was no longer necessary to be Aboriginal. 'On the streets of New York I might have been from anywhere — South America, Greece, Italy — and the racism wasn't directed against me' (1996: 98). The UN enabled him to be 'a citizen of the world' (1996: 98). Wayne relished a Bangladesh posting, with its good pay and the opportunities that he made for learning that other international language, French. Yet, after returning to New York he felt discontented, and in 1975 he resigned and went back to Sydney. As soon as he arrived, he knew he had made a mistake, for to be back in Australia was to be an Aboriginal person once more. Taking a job as a court reporter, he heard the room go quiet when he answered his new work-mates' questions about where he was from; the subsequent conversations about 'the Aboriginal problem' were a disheartening reminder of white Australian complacency. He worked as hard as he could to save the fare that took him back to New York in March 1976. 'This time I wouldn't come back to Australia. I would never come back to Australia. I knew I didn't belong. I would be a gypsy for the rest of my life' (1996: 125).

Wayne King found New York and Ismailia (outside Cairo) — his next United Nations posting — to be truly cosmopolitan spaces; people from many countries and of many colours worked side by side and among these work-mates there was simply no category 'Aboriginal' available to apply to him. He became friendly with the only gay work-mate, an Argentine called Alfredo, and they mixed with a group of gay diplomats whose social outings would always begin by a discussion about which language they would use that night.

In the richest sense of the word, Wayne's happiness in Egypt was the product of his 'deracination'. Over several years, he had thoroughly uprooted himself from a culture in which he and his kind were the object of racism. He lived in a world that was relatively autonomous from the person-defining processes of family and nation. One word that describes this semi-detached world is 'impersonal'; here was 'impersonality' in a benign form, the demands and opportunities of international bureaucracy and of gay sexuality combining to foster an ethos of personal liberty.

This turned out to be not enough for Wayne King, and his story makes it impossible to romanticise 'deracination'; he makes us see the limitations, for him, of the UN's cosmopolitan impersonality. He became alcoholic and psychotic, and this prompted him to come back to Australia and to hear his mother's life history. *Black Hours* is one of those Indigenous autobiographies — the most famous is Sally Morgan's *My Place* (1987) — in which the narrator discovers a part of the truth of him or herself in the narrative of a parent's or grandparent's suffering. As he puts it, 'I came back to Australia to find my roots. But I found my roots had been taken from me' (1996: 224). In that low state, a friend persuades him to join Alcoholics Anonymous, and the book ends with Wayne urging that Australians take a step towards national maturity by ceasing to deny their collective racism.

Concluding Comments

In each of these autobiographies, an Aboriginal man is enabled to see himself in new ways partly by his experience of being a public servant. There is a way to think about the impersonality of bureaucracy that assumes that impersonality is the nemesis of 'personality', as if the 'machine' necessarily tends to obliterate the person. Charles Perkins' account comes closest to saying something like this. Becoming a 'paper warrior' confines him; and he is impatient, and even dismissive, of the established procedures of financial administration and recruitment. Yet his attitude to 'impersonality' is on the whole more complex and ambivalent. When he reproaches the diplomats who failed to help him, he invokes an ethic of selfless pubic service, and he is in no doubt that Aborigines must learn to use the machinery of government, whether it be a Department of Aboriginal Affairs reconstituted as a statutory authority or their own publicly subsidised organisations. He joined the public service to learn its techniques, and as readers we know that he had thirteen years as a senior public servant after publishing his account of his initiation.

Gordon Matthews narrates his personal quest for the truth of his heritage partly according to the trope that impersonality is the nemesis of personality; I am thinking of his reluctance to reveal to his boss his discovery that he is in fact Sri Lankan-Australian, not Aboriginal-Australian, as if the machine would judge him as dishonouring its investment in him as an Aborigine. But his public service boss is not troubled by having quietly to change a line in Gordon's personal file. Not only did impersonal administration allow him to be 'Aboriginal' and even to reward him for being so; it was no less forgiving of his ceasing to be 'Aboriginal'. Bureaucratic impersonality turns out to be accommodating of 'difference'; it can choose to inscribe and re-inscribe ethnicity as merely the private characteristic of a functional person.

Finally, Wayne King allows us to see one of the limits of this accommodating impersonality. There is something enabling and something disabling about an ethos that does not care who you are. In the world of the floating UN bureaucrat, especially in that version of its *socialities* that gay men are able to perform, to be deracinated is both emancipating and deeply unsatisfying, at least for someone such as Wayne King who is in a condition of existentially insecure flight from the roots of his social being.

These three books give us a glimpse of the potential of administrative memoirs to be essays in the psychology of contemporary Australian liberalism.

Writing Political Biography

Rae Wear

Writing political biography almost always involves a degree of self-exploration: there is a little bit of autobiography lurking beneath the surface of every biography. To begin with, there is the choice of subject. Some biographers are drawn to personalities they admire while others tackle those they have little regard for but consider important or perhaps want to understand. Choosing a subject must involve reflection on the biographer's part about the reasons for their choice and also about the nature of the feelings they bring to the task. This reflection is essential if a biography is to be other than hagiography or a hatchet job. In my own choice of subject, Johannes Bjelke-Petersen, I was driven by a desire to understand the community in which I had lived most of my life and which had played a large part in my own political socialisation. Bjelke-Petersen was a man who had both shaped that community and been shaped by it. In growing up in provincial Queensland I had become acquainted with many of Bjelke-Petersen's men and women who in many respects were kindly churchgoers, yet who would think nothing of rorting their tax or doing slippery business deals. They always puzzled me, as Bjelke-Petersen did — that combination of rectitude and shady dealings.

I therefore set out with opinions ready formed. I had studied sufficient Queensland politics to know of his reputation for authoritarianism, contempt for Parliament and due process, rigging of the electoral system, and of the persistent rumours of corruption. In a timid and law-abiding fashion I had participated in protests against his curtailment of civil liberties in Queensland. The task for me as for any biographer was to try to understand him, and his success, rather than to give vent to the negative feelings I had accumulated. I imagine the obverse is true for those who set out to write about someone they admire. In trying to understand comes the recognition that the subject is a complex figure, neither all good nor all bad. Finding skeletons in the cupboard of an admired figure may be more difficult for a biographer to deal with than finding a human spark in a subject previously reviled.

There is a great deal of artifice in the biographer's work. A life is packaged, a story told, loose ends snipped off. The story is told as if it is *the* story. I have often wondered about applying to biography the device used in Akira Kurosawa's famous film *Rashomon* and the novels that comprise Laurence Durrell's *Alexandria Quartet*. These works describe the same events from multiple viewpoints and highlight the difficulty associated with producing a 'true' version of anything. A reliable biographer takes account of conflicting points of view, and checks and confirms data, but in the end the form demands a coherent and well ordered package which never mirrors the messiness of a subject's life. In my own work, I tried to convey some of the complexity of my subject's life by avoiding an historical narrative and examining Bjelke-Petersen's premiership through a series of relationships with a range of political institutions. I found, however, that historical narrative crept in through the back door, so I do not judge this to be a totally successful strategy

This problem of dealing with a range of conflicting viewpoints about a subject may be exacerbated by the use of interviews. Both James Walter and Judith Brett have written admirable biographies without doing interviews although, as Brett points out in the Introduction to *Political Lives,* some critics took them to task about this. Not using interviews certainly removes a lot of static, and means that a biographer is relying for evidence on stable historical sources rather than on frequently biased, unreliable and frequently unverifiable recollections. Interviewing the subjects' friends, enemies, acquaintances and colleagues inevitably places the biographer in a *Rashomon*-like situation, where all and sundry present their truthful but conflicting points of view. It may be the case that some interviewees try deliberately to mislead but I believe they are in the minority. Most people tell the story as they see it, but they rarely see the same thing because they have experienced different facets of a subject's personality. Bjelke-Petersen, for example, appeared to be benign and kindly until he was crossed. His supporters remain intensely loyal and appear never to have seen his angry and vindictive side. Reconciling divergent views about a subject does make the biographer's task difficult. Matters of fact can be checked, and the interviewee's relationship with the subject taken into account to try to establish the truth of the matter, but it is a challenge to present a multi-faceted personality in a coherent fashion and not lose the multi-faceted quality.

Sometimes I felt compromised by having accepted an interviewee's hospitality. In no case was this any more than a cup of tea and a slice of cake, but it made it so much harder to be critical. Bjelke-Petersen was famous for disarming his critics. Bob Ellis in *Goodbye Jerusalem* describes how he was absolutely enchanted by Sir Joh during a visit to Bethany, the Bjelke-Petersen property. In my own book I retell a story told by the late Andrew Olle who, as a current affairs reporter, accompanied Sir Joh on a flight to the Torres Strait. Andrew mentioned that he would have to make an early start the following morning, and was greeted at sunrise by the premier bearing a cup of tea. Undoubtedly Bjelke-Petersen had learnt the advantages that such actions can bring. As Pat Weller has observed, contacts of this kind reveal the human side of the interviewee and these glimpses of humanity are what can make it so hard to be a critic. I think this is true, but the act of 'breaking bread' and accepting hospitality compounds the problem.

Considering all this, is it worth doing interviews especially when there is the added consideration that politicians are adept at avoiding giving much away in interviews? This is particularly true of serving politicians and I would probably never bother interviewing them for the purpose of biography. Sometimes, however, politicians become more expansive in retirement. Occasionally they feel they 'want to get matters on to the public record' or, more often, they want to settle old political scores. Sometimes some interesting insights emerge that have never been committed to the written record. Certainly interview material can add colour, interest and the occasional quirky gem. My own favourite from the Bjelke-Petersen biography came from an interview with the premier's first media adviser, Hugh Bingham:

> I was sitting in the nice little premier's dining room and the cook came in with this beautiful tureen. The table was beautifully set with wine glasses and he lifted up the top of the tureen and it was boiled pumpkin and potatoes. Beautifully set out. They were just flawless. Absolutely flawless pumpkins and potatoes.

The image of those flawless vegetables has stayed with me with their revelations of the premier's asceticism, and the trappings of power.

Biography is a difficult craft. While there are many good political biographies, there are very few great ones. Too often it seems that years of careful research fail to grasp the subject's elusive essence. Fiction often seems to do a better job of this. For example, none of the biographies of Huey Long that I have read captures the man's essence nearly as well as Robert Penn Warren's *All the King's Men* (1946). A similar comment was made about my book *Johannes Bjelke-Petersen, the Lord's Premier* (2002). One reviewer observed that Andrew McGahan's *Last Drinks* (2000) captures the politics Bjelke-Petersen's Queensland more effectively than my own book. I think he may have been right, but at this point I can only reply that I was not writing fiction. Next time, though, I would like to bring something more to the process of political biography, and be a little more adventurous in marrying art with craft.

Jessie Street and the New Political Biography

Lenore Coltheart

Most political biographies of women are about female heads of state, heads of government, and parliamentary representatives, but most women who have exercised power on political structures and processes have done so as non-government actors. An expanded definition of political biography brings in these unofficial figures who 'impacted on policy, politics or government'. We probably should consider, too, the reverse vectors, as the influence of the geopolitical is too frequently understated in writing lives, as if these could ever be immune from either national politics or international relations. So political biography has much to teach across the whole field of the biographer, from the famous to the family historian and the appearance, largely since 1990, of political biographies of 'unofficial' women is encouraging. Books on women suffragists paved the way for more recent work like those on Marietta Tree, Shirley Graham Du Bois, Grace Hutchins and Anna Rochester (Seebohm, 1997; Horne, 2000; Lee, 2000), for example, which bring a diverse range of women within the political penumbra. Such work suggests a shift in feminist history, as well as in the study of politics, towards more contextual explanation of flows of power between public and private lives.

The subject of my work is feminist internationalist Jessie Street. Street died in 1970 at the age of 80. I had started work on a study of connections between the humanitarian work of the League of Nations and the human rights functions of the United Nations Economic & Social Council. Specifically I was interested in Australian women and the influence of NGOs on this work. It was not long before I encountered Jessie Street and she took over my project. She had thirty years of experience within the international network of women's NGOs, from her first visit to the League in Geneva in 1930 until her last UN session in New York in the 1960s. And I met her through two excellent publications. *The Australian Dictionary of Biography* is an invaluable resource for political biographers, but I want also to mention Heather Radi's *200 Australian Women* (1988). The splendid index in this book reveals connections not always obvious in other Australian politics resources. Tracing vectors of influence between people and through organisational networks is every bit as important in what might be called 'non-government' political biography, as when the subject was officially a political actor. Perhaps Jim Walter's term, 'organic intellectual', can be adapted and the non-official figures be considered organic political actors.

A year after I realised the work I was doing was turning into biography, I had a request from Jessie Street's family to do a revision of her 1966 autobiography, *Truth or Repose*. Like many others — including the prospective publisher — I thought initially this was not really a useful exercise, and perhaps not even possible. But the challenge was there and, while convincing the publisher, I convinced myself. The work of 'ghost-revising' an autobiography was an unusual task with the pragmatic advantage of making me live a lot closer with Jessie Street and able to talk frequently with her elder daughter, who generously read draft chapters and provided invaluable support. There were good and bad spin-offs. Soaking myself in my subject's own words made me realise how much she had needed a research assistant and a good editor — and then I knew just how to approach the work — but it took much longer than I had allowed. The new book also drew attention to this remarkable woman rather too soon for my own work to squeeze into the arc of media attention. But, for me, the premature publicity drew out unexpected angles of current opinion on Jessie Street and her story. ABC TV did a *New Dimensions* segment they called 'Radicals and Reformers' in 2003 and the following year the ABC *Dynasties* team could not resist giving her a large chunk of their episode on the Street law dynasty, so far a male preserve dominated by three Chief Justices of the NSW Supreme Court. The book's publication in March 2004 brought requests for interviews and talks, including Gerard Henderson's irresistible invitation to speak at the Sydney Institute on 'that dreadful Stalinist Jessie Street'.

Through the diversion of the new edition of the autobiography I came closer to knowing why I wanted to write a biography. The 'how' of the biography is more straightforward. Unusually for an unofficial political figure, a woman working through women's organisations, Jessie Street left a pretty good archival trail. There are copious files of official and personal letters, some diaries, lots of private and formal photographs, and many transcripts of speeches and broadcasts and drafts of articles. There is also a newspaper trail, presenting several Jessie Streets — from 1947 a 'Red Jessie' emerges. This Jessie Street also appears in ministerial minutes and memos, the asides on government records that reveal much about attitudes, and this same 'Red Jessie' is presented in her very substantial ASIO files.

As well as the archival trail, there are diverse informal discoveries from family and colleagues, both material and oral evidence. Place is also important — particularly Yulgilbar, the property on the upper Clarence River in northern New South Wales where Jessie Street grew up. Equally important are the international trails. A three month trip in 2004 took me to possibly half the places she regularly visited or that were significant to her work, like San Francisco for instance. From April to June 1945 the Australian delegation to the conference setting up the United Nations stayed in the Sir Francis Drake Hotel. Unhappily, hotels are very bad at keeping guest register records for sixty years, but it was a great discovery to find that the hotel's English theme lived on, including doormen in beefeater rig. In New York I prowled Manhattan's lower East Side to find locations like the former girls' home where Jessie Street had worked in 1915. Washington, the headquarters of the World Women's Party where Jessie Street worked with Alice Paul from the 1930s, has now become an invaluable archive and museum.

Only half awake and exhausted after a jet-lagged sleep on my first morning in San Francisco, I stood waiting in the June dawn for the cable car outside the hotel thinking the Australian delegation in 1945 had taken two days to reach San Francisco, travelling under wartime conditions that included flying only at night. Suddenly I realised Jessie Street had stood where I stood. Despite the obvious changes to the city, all of it — my exhaustion the night before, my excitement on waking, the chilly sunrise, the gorgeous June sky, called up a similar day sixty years before. It was a good start on a discovery of the effect place has, a pointer to how biographical research needs to cross over methodological boundaries.

It was catching that idea that also attuned me to taking a more materialist approach. It became a lot easier to imagine my subject in a room, with details of curtains and chairs, her clothes, her bag of files and newspapers. The train station in Budapest in 1938, Le Bourget airport in 1951, the material surrounds of her travelling took shape. The vital issue of money has already been raised — Jessie Street's bank accounts and the fact that it was her own money she paid out is significant in explaining her profile in international NGO networks. Everything about everyday life including eating, drinking, smoking — when, how, with whom — are details not to be overlooked. If I was asked to paint a portrait of the objects most familiar to Jessie Street's everyday life, I could just about do it — a telephone, a bunch of the day's newspapers and her glasses, her passport and an airline ticket, her cigarettes and lighter, her capacious handbag full of files, her cameo brooch, her tiny diary full of scribbled appointments, her address book arranged by country, and a gift for someone, wrapped and ready to send.

It is with such details that real world connections can be caught in life stories. This is particularly important for the political biographer whose subject held no public political position. Jessie Street's work was done mostly through non-government organisations and international networks of women. As in any political biography her work can only be explained in the context of contemporary national and international political events, but with the unofficial activist, the big-picture context tends to sever detailed connections within private lives.

Questions that require evidence both from political history and from personal history are key points for remaking the connections of lives lived in a political context. Jessie Street failed to be elected to parliament and was stripped of her government appointments, so how she built power bases before and after these events is a key question. This kind of question means drilling down for detail while keeping antenna tuned to the broadest issues — like why is a power base necessary to participate in politics when this is what democracy is meant to offer for all of us? Issues central to biographies of official figures have this double effect when the subject is an 'organic' political figure working less visibly through cultural, rather than government channels. Asking how power is lost and what happens after it is lost similarly connects public events and personal issues, as does the big calculation, assessing the achievements and failures of one's subject. Peter Sekuless subtitled his 1978 biography of Jessie Street *A Rewarding but Unrewarded Life*, a title almost as inappropriate a motif for Jessie Street as the one she gave to her autobiography, *Truth or Repose* (1966). Maybe both matters would have been sorted had she used the title she first thought of: 'God I've had a lovely life'.

A life like Jessie Street's challenges the managerialist approach to political biography, counting goals met, agendas fulfilled and targets 'bullseyed' to rate the subject. Among the problems confronting the 'organic' political biographer is how to sum up and how to tie off so many threads of detail and big-picture banners. Perhaps the means is the end: the process of participating makes a political life. In this light, the non-government women activists whose work shaped the development of human rights in the twentieth century grew a form of international citizenship that can be conferred no other way but through its practice.

A life like Jessie Street's means following research paths that seem to lead in opposite directions, but perhaps this is the best way to attach political science, history, and international relations more firmly to life as we know it.

Conjuring Fascinating Stories: the Case of Sir Arthur Tange

Peter Edwards

Shortly after Frank Crowley, then lecturing in history at the University of Western Australia, started his biography of John Forrest, he confronted his second-year students with a question: 'It is said that every historian should tackle a biography at some stage in his life. What do you think?' As I recall, the second-year students sat there with their mouths opening and closing silently like dyspeptic goldfish. One of them, however, for some reason remembered that remark. Thirty years later I recalled it when I was trying to work out what my next project should be, having just worked on the official history of Australia's involvement in Malaya, Borneo and Vietnam, as well as various other projects. I wanted to do something which built on that work but which was also different. I thought that tackling a biography would be of interest. It occurred to me that somebody really ought to do a biography of the public servant Arthur Tange, a person to whom many historians, myself included, had referred with a one-word summary, either 'legendary' or 'formidable'.

Arthur Tange was a lifelong public servant. Public service to him was more than a career; it was, I think, a vocation. He had the unusual experience of being what was called a First Division officer for more than a quarter of a century — eleven years as the Secretary of the Department of External Affairs (1954–65); a diplomatic appointment as High Commissioner to India and Ambassador to Nepal (1965–70); and then $9\frac{1}{2}$ years as Secretary of the Department of Defence (1970–79).

So, after various negotiations, I am now writing a biography. I am also editing a memoir that Tange himself wrote late in his life, mostly focused on his period in Defence. There is a third part to the project as well. I organised and prepared a list of his papers for the National Library. So, if you now go, as I hope many of you will, to consult MS9847 in the Manuscripts Collection, you will be reading a different sort of publication of mine.

Political scientists these days, we have been told, talk a lot about triangulation. Historians like to talk about memory — how do we construct memory and what is the interaction between individual memory and collective memory. So there is a certain dimension in that conversation to be gained from simultaneously ordering the remarkably chaotic and disorganised papers of a bureaucrat; looking at what he wrote about himself; and writing his biography.

Why write about a senior bureaucrat? It seems to me fairly straightforward. Tange's career peaked in a particular period, between two major revolutions in the public service and the way the public service operated. This first occurred during the Second World War, the second started under the Whitlam Government, with sequels under the Hawke and Keating governments. That period, roughly the 1940s to the 1970s, was the era of the great 'mandarins' of the public service. It is no coincidence that it was also the time of great institution-building in government, the development of major public service departments.

I have conjured up a rather fanciful image of how policy was actually formed on major issues during that time, and particularly during the long Menzies period. One can compare, I think, Menzies with a sort of medieval monarch in his court, surrounded by various barons, they being the major ministers and also the major heads of department, with certain fluctuating coalitions and combinations forming. And what formed a really powerful combination was if there was a politically powerful minister with a powerful, bureaucratically astute public servant at the head of his department. The classic example would be John McEwen and John Crawford as respectively Minister and Secretary of the Department of Trade.

In writing the biography there have been various stakeholders whose interests I have to consider and balance. There is firstly the subject himself. I have had an unusual experience concerning the question of whether to write on a living or deceased subject. Arthur Tange was alive when I started work and he is now dead. But his son and daughter are very much alive, and I have had to consider that. The project has also been supported by the Department of Defence. That department and the Department of Foreign Affairs and Trade are, despite their reputations for secrecy and a consciousness of security, among the most generous and liberal sponsors of histories. That includes, not just their own history (such as David Day has done for Customs), but also histories of topics within their general field. It is something that other public service departments might do well to follow.

I like asking political science-type questions. Many of my interests are to do with the interaction of institutions and individuals and how power is gained, how power is exercised, how policy is made. I have tried to combine those interests into something of interest to that mythical character, beloved of publishers, the 'interested general reader'.

The four major themes are nicely alliterative: policy, politics, public administration and personality. I simply do not think one can understand how major policy decisions in this period emerge without understanding the interaction between ministers and senior public servants at this time. Pat Weller made the comment some time ago that if the mandarins wanted to claim the credit for all the things that went right in that period, they had to take some of the blame for what went wrong. It is a fair comment. My response would be that, in many cases, what we now see as successful examples of policy-making and policy creation were cases when ministers and their top public servants worked very effectively together, each knowing and understanding what the other could and could not do. In the period that I am dealing with, the cases included the negotiation of the ANZUS Treaty and the Colombo Plan, the handling of Indonesian confrontation in the 1960s, and the reorganisation of strategic policy in the 1970s. On the other hand, what we now generally see as policy failures, such as the 1956 Suez crisis, or the discussions that led to Australian involvement in Vietnam in 1965, were cases where there was a disjunction between the top level public servants and the ministers. There was distrust, there was sidelining, there was exclusion, there was simply not the collaboration that marks good minister–official relations.

Politics in the sense that we often use that term, the sort of stuff that feeds the headlines of the newspapers, does not figure prominently in this account. Public servants themselves are not supposed to be involved in that sort of thing. It does so happen, however, that Tange was a little more involved than he wished, albeit unwittingly, in the downfall of John Gorton as prime minister. There is also the theory, repeatedly alleged by certain journalists in the 1970s and 1980s, that Arthur Tange was the evil genius who was the link between the security crisis and the constitutional crisis in late 1975. According to this story, Tange was the person who told Sir John Kerr that the CIA was worried about the Whitlam Government, thus contributing substantially to the dismissal. I have taken that story out of the main body of my narrative. An appendix in the book discusses what Tange did or did not do in 1975 on the security crisis, the constitutional crisis and the third largely simultaneous crisis, the covert Indonesian invasion of East Timor leading to the death of five Australia-based journalists at Balibo.

There is a close relationship between policy structures, policy-making structures and policy outcomes. That would seem to be fairly straightforward, although it is a little subtler than the familiar American political science dictum, 'where you stand depends upon where you sit'. I interviewed, among many other people, Gough Whitlam or, as he preferred to say, he granted me an audience. Soon after that experience, I pressed the button on my telephone answering machine. That very familiar voice emerged: 'The trouble with you, Peter, is you take the departmental view'. It was not meant as a compliment but I in fact took it as one because I took it as confirmation that there is such a thing as the 'departmental view'. Tange's achievement in developing a professional foreign office and diplomatic service out of what had been a rather disparate bunch of more or less talented individuals led to the creation of something that could be called a 'departmental line' in foreign policy. This was different from either the standard party line of either the Coalition parties or the Labor Party. The interaction of these various lines is what has led to some of our most interesting policy decisions.

Tange is best remembered now for the so-called Tange reforms of Defence in the 1970s, when five departments were merged into one. This not only raised many issues about civil–military relations and the merger of three services into one Australian Defence Force. It is also closely related to the strategic policies associated with phrases like 'self-reliance' and 'the defence of Australia', concepts now coming under serious challenge for the first time.

It is impossible to talk of Tange without discussing his personality. Stories about Tange in his day were legion throughout Canberra and the public service, especially stories of his confrontations with public servants, throwing files down in front of them so the unfortunate officer would have to scramble on the floor to pick up the disarrayed papers. There were his telephone conversations where, as he sometimes said, 'I have to strike like lightning'. What I want to discuss is the effect that his personality had on the operations of his departments. Did it help to generate good policy discussion or did it constrict policy-making?

To bring these themes together, I have structured the book around the theme of the relationship between ministers and mandarins. The most interesting question, from this period of great mandarins, is what made for good, productive relationships between a minister and the head of department and what made for dysfunctional relationships. Tange, as he liked to claim, was very proud of having directly served 17 ministers and five prime ministers. So he had the full range of experience, from one that was almost a filial, father-son relationship to one verging on open hostility. What was it that made for good relationships, what was it that did not?

It does occur to me that somebody might like to make one of those docu-dramas of the relationship between Tange and Hasluck from their days as undergraduates at UWA in the 1930s through to the 1980s as retired gentlemen, full of years and honours. It would make a fascinating story. I am sure that if Geoffrey Bolton (Hasluck's latest biographer) and I were consultants on such an episode, we would collaborate rather better than Tange and Hasluck did in 1965.

This biography has taken me into a variety of areas, in order to discuss Tange's public and private life. I necessarily discuss matters such as income and family life, including his relations with his children. There is not as much about his sex life as might be expected by a culture obsessed with who is sleeping with whom, but I do not think that is a huge weakness. I do have to touch on numerous historical fields, other than foreign and defence policy. One is immigration history, since one side of his forebears came from Denmark and the other from Britain, in fact the Anglo–Irish Ascendancy. One gets into sports history, because the different roles of rugby union in New South Wales and in Western Australia come into this story. One gets into economic history and banking history, because an early mentor of Tange's, a relation by marriage, was Sir Alfred Davidson, the influential head of the Bank of New South Wales in the 1930s and 1940s. One touches on a matter raised earlier in this workshop, concerning the development of a common ethos among international civil servants, particularly around the late 1940s. The first air trip that Arthur Tange ever made — he never liked air trips very much — was in a DC4 flying over the Pacific during wartime to a little-known place in New Hampshire called Bretton Woods.

In this biography I have tried to bring together these themes, to answer questions in a way that I hope will be not only useful to political scientists, not least those in this room, but also of interest to many other Australians. If you will forgive the cliché, there is a fascinating Australian story behind it all.

Anonymous in Life, Anonymous in Death: Memoirs and Biographies of Administrators

John Nethercote

This essay has two objectives: the first is to provide a *tour d'horizon* of biographies and autobiographies of administrators. Its second purpose is to comment on the utility of biography as a method of studying administration and its contribution to government.

In comparison with political leaders and the more public figures in government and politics, Australian administrators are not well-served by biographies, even in the brief form found in the *Australian Dictionary of Biography* . There is a great reluctance to engage with these officials as 'subjects' for biography and reluctance among officials to consider writing autobiographical memoirs. This is true elsewhere. If we examine British history, it is well-known that Sir Geoffrey Elton, the doyen of Tudor studies, notoriously refused to write a biography of Thomas Cromwell, the minister-bureaucrat behind such a great event as the Reformation in England, although Elton's contemporary, A.G. Dickens, eventually undertook the task in a volume still worth reading (1959).

There is no biography of the legendary founder of the modern British civil service, Sir Charles Trevelyan. Bare details of his career may be found in the *ODNB*, and some of his accomplishments in Maurice Wright's classic, *Treasury control of the Civil Service, 1854-1874* (1969). To learn about Trevelyan's character readers must go to Trollope's *Three Clerks*,(2004 [1858]) where he appears as 'Sir Gregory Hardlines'. The authenticity of the novelist's portrait is attested by Lady Trevelyan, who confided to Trollope that in her home they sometimes referred to Sir Charles as 'Sir Gregory'. Trevelyan's great twentieth century counterpart, Sir Warren Fisher, is one of the few administrators to have hurdled the biographical barrier.

In the mid-twentieth century, there are a host of books on Winston Churchill especially on the conduct of his war-time prime ministership. But virtually missing from most of these endeavours is the civilian support for Churchill during those years provided by Sir Edward Bridges, though his contribution was immense. Bridges' role in government has been only selectively addressed (Chapman 1988).

By contrast, the most famous administrator in British history, Samuel Pepys, has had more books — and generally better books — written about him than all

Australian prime ministers put together. Pepys's own diaries run to ten volumes and cover only the decade of the 1660s.

In Australia there is a small library of biographies and autobiographies about and by officials from the foreign and defence services. Among heads of Foreign Affairs, apart from Peter Edwards' life of Sir Arthur Tange (2006), and Sir Arthur's own memoirs (1996), there have been autobiographies from Sir Alan Watt (1972), Alan Renouf (1980), Peter Henderson (1986), and Richard Woolcott (2003) as well as several ambassadors —Alf Stirling (1973), Jim Cumes (1988) and Ralph Harry (1983). Fin Crisp wrote an insightful recollection of his friend Sir Peter Heydon, Secretary of Immigration, 1960–71 (1972), and a biography of Sir James Plimsoll is in preparation. David Horner has composed a major study of Sir Frederick Shedden, head of Defence from the mid-1930s to the mid-1950s (2000).

Otherwise Australia's main administrative biographical studies of are of two veterans — H.C. 'Nugget' Coombs and John Crawford — from the Department of Postwar Reconstruction, an organisation with a considerable reputation in its day and since for self-publicity.

Among the notable autobiographical memoirs, sometimes revealing in ways the authors may not have intended, are Coombs's *Trial Balance* (1981), Robert Garran's *Prosper the Commonwealth* (1958), Sir William Dunk's *They Also Serve* (1974), John Menadue's *Things You Learn Along the Way* (1999) and Alf Rattigan's *Industry Assistance: The inside story* (1986).

The most pronounced gaps on the administrative biography shelf are Sir Robert Garran and Sir Roland Wilson. Garran was unquestionably the major figure in administration in the first three decades of the Commonwealth and his influence extended well beyond the field of law to imperial and international relations, the workings of the federation, the structure of the public service and the ever-vexatious field of industrial relations. Sir Roland Wilson was instrumental in the development, at a critical time, of three major institutions of Australian government — the Australian Bureau of Statistics, the Department of Labour and National Service (now the Department of Employment and Workplace Relations), and the Treasury (including the Department of Finance). As a long-serving board member of the Commonwealth Bank, the Reserve Bank and QANTAS, including extended periods as chairman of two of them, he was a major contributor to the practice of public enterprise in Australia's Keynesian era. Not only is there not a scholarly biography of Roland Wilson, for reasons (it has been said) of caprice he was not even the subject of an essay in the Reserve Bank-funded book on leading financiers in Australia, though few had greater claims to a place than he.

For administrators, it seems that that badge of their profession, anonymity, follows them not only in their 'official life' and in retirement but also in death.

Yet administrators and their institutions have played an integral part in Australia's history. The testimony of Second World War historian, Sir Paul Hasluck, is instructive:

> In writing the civil volumes of the official war history I took the view that the person who bears the political responsibility for action should be credited with having taken the action. Now, in a more personal account of the war years, I take the liberty of passing on most of the credit for war-time administration to the senior public servants.

> … looking only at its daily administration a few public servants carried the burden nobly almost in spite of their ministers. The war effort was managed to a large extent by them.

Their 'life studies' would be valuable and should be encouraged. Johnson's dictum should be recalled: that 'there has rarely passed a life of which a judicious and faithful narrative would not be useful'. In Johnson's view, knowledge of 'mistakes and miscarriages, escapes and expedients' are likely to be 'of immediate and, apparent use'. Acknowledging the value of life studies, however, still leaves open questions of form, length and scope. Donne's precept, that no man is an island unto himself, applies with greater force to administrators than politicians and many other professions.

Administration is quintessentially a collegial activity — though the collegiality will often be exceedingly competitive (see Hasluck 1980: 159). In the past as in the present there are few opportunities for an administrator to place an individual stamp on a policy or an institution. Because of his youth, and the fact that he was present at the creation of Federation, Garran had an unusual career; nonetheless, for the first decade and a half of his long secretaryship in the Attorney-General's Department, it would be necessary to give due weight to the influence of other comparable figures, Atlee Hunt, at External Affairs, Woolaston at Trade and Customs, and the mighty Duncan McLachlan, the inaugural Public Service Commissioner. But by the Second World War and the subsequent periods of reconstruction, affluence and prosperity, it is difficult for any one individual to claim an uncontested ascendancy. To focus on an individual may well prove to be an act of considerable distortion at several levels, including of the subject individual.

While many officials (and, indeed, politicians) are worthy of study, few warrant an 80,000 word monograph. Quite a number, however, justify more than the thousand or so words for which they might qualify if selected for an entry in the *Australian Dictionary of Biography* .

In the case of officialdom, there is a strong argument for greater use of the essay as the principal form of biography. The essay has an honourable place in the history of biography. It was essentially the form used by the Roman chronicler

life, their pre-political life, their time after politics (in some cases) and to other interests outside the purely political. The politician's autobiography is usually a more introspective book than the political autobiography.

The classic Australian politician's autobiography of recent years is Bill Hayden's, *Hayden: an Autobiography* (1996). As I wrote elsewhere, 'at its worst the reader feels he is beside the psychotherapist's couch, at its best there is a raw, unflinching honesty about the book, about his personal life as well as his political life'.

I include the 'political memoir' out of deference to my colleague, John Button. Button has apparently skipped across life and politics so disarmingly — 'dodging raindrops' indeed — that he is too elusive to categorise. So I surrender to his own definition of his book, *As It Happened* (1998), which he describes as 'a memoir rather than an autobiography'. In Button's words, talking particularly about the political side, the political memoir, 'is not the full bottle … it lacks the historian's discipline of poring over archives [providing] an account that seems to include everything'. The political aspect of the political memoir lacks the authority and comprehensiveness of a political autobiography or a politician's autobiography. There is no sense that armies of research students have been mobilised as they were for Hawke's book and, I suspect, for Hayden's, to provide the factual material and do the research to back up their claims. The political memoir is much more lightly done.

Moreover, in relation to the private side, Button himself admits that *his* political memoir omits 'things in my life … which in different degrees have been more important than anything else in my life'. Thus, on the personal side, the political memoir is more lightweight than the politician's autobiography as it is more lightweight on the political side than the political autobiography. Skipping lightly across events therefore makes the political memoir the most elegant of these forms. Robert Menzies' *Afternoon Light* (1967) is a classic and elegiac example of the political memoir.

The 'political diary' is a distinct form of writing by a politician. It is usually as relentlessly political, often obsessively so, as the political autobiography. Most political diarists concentrate very much on the detail of the political life. Indeed, if you think of the classic modern examples — Richard Crossman (1975-77), Castle (1980), Howson (1984), Tony Benn (1987-1992), and even my own work — there is very little in any of these books about the personal lives of the writers. The diaries of all these politicians include fleeting references to their private lives but remain overwhelmingly political. Alan Clark (1993-2002) comes to mind as a possible exception — his enthusiastic accounts of his extra-political activities are compelling but, then, Clark is *sui generis* among contemporary political diarists.

The political diary is usually aimed at political junkies. It tends to be dense with material, often in a pretty undigested form. There is not much selectivity, often for very good reasons, and is often, as a result, rather turgid.

The political diary is usually written by a member of the second eleven, or at least the lower half of the first eleven, that is by people who have the time to observe and to write their observations down. One review of my diary suggested I was 'an interested bystander', which is partly the point I am making. Another said that I was 'an observant fly on the Cabinet wall'. One of my colleagues suggested, tersely, if you substituted 'blowfly' for 'fly', you would be closer to the mark.

One should not underrate the advantages of the political diary. One great advantage is that it has an immediacy that most of the other forms of political writing lack, particularly if they are kept, as mine was, on a daily basis. As a result of this immediacy you learn about events before they collect the mythology that transforms them. I will give one example, 24 February 1992, the encounter between Paul Keating and Queen Elizabeth II, around which a vast mythology has accreted. This is simply my view that night of what happened.

There was a gathering of the political elite in the Great Hall of the Parliament to meet the Queen. There was also rather unseemly pressure, indeed a lot of pushing from Labor republicans — or rather from their wives — to be introduced to the Queen. Keating was much more dignified, relaxed and assured than he was with Bush, striking a restrained note of independence in his speech and guiding the Queen with aplomb through the milling hordes.

His guiding of the Queen through the throng became, in the British tabloids, 'The Lizard of Oz mauls our Queen'. There is something to be said for getting a record of events before they are subject to hyperbole.

Most autobiographical writing by politicians is dismayingly dogmatic — in part because they possess the great advantage of hindsight. You do not have that gift with a daily diary. On the eve of the 1993 election I wrote:

> Of all the elections I have been involved in, this one I have found the most difficult to read. My instinct tells me we will lose: ten years and one million unemployed are a coincidence we can hardly survive. But my head and the polls suggest we may well win. This dilemma arises, I suspect, because I cannot factor in the effect of our own scare campaign. Are there, in total, enough groups out there sufficiently antagonised by one or more of the Hewson horrors to give us a slim majority? Tomorrow will tell. (Blewett 1999)

In political diaries the future is unknown, outcomes uncertain. In Hawke's autobiography, by contrast, we would find something like this: 'As always I accurately predicted the outcome'; or, in Hayden's writing, something like this:

'Though convulsed by doubts I believed we would win'. Uncertainty is a characteristic of the political diary.

Moreover, in a political diary, not only is there uncertainty but the writer can get things plain wrong. For six years I have suffered ridicule for the last paragraph in *A Cabinet Diary*. On the evening of the election I wrote:

> Keating claimed victory in a euphoric and apparently unprepared speech. 'This is the sweetest victory of all' And so it is. With luck it has opened the nineties to Labor and all the tough decisions of the last few years will now bring their rewards ... Tomorrow belongs to us. (Blewett 1999)

There are constraints on writing and publishing political diaries, particularly those by ministers. These constraints should be seen in the light of the two golden commandments for diarists:

1. thou shalt not alter entries as a result of hindsight; and
2. thou shalt not bowdlerise or soften the original entries.

If one wants to be a decent diarist these seem to me to be sacred commands.

As with all commandments these encounter difficulties in the real world. The first of these is that unlike political autobiographies, politician's autobiographies or political memoirs, where politicians seem to be able to discuss debates in cabinet without any serious concerns — look, for example, at Hawke and Peter Walsh — the political diary is seen differently, as somehow subversive, more dangerous than other kinds of political writing.

Censorship has been invoked against political diaries in the latter part of the twentieth century. Crossman (1975-77) had to fight a court battle to get his diaries published. I had the following warning shot across my bow when I indicated to the Department of the Prime Minister and Cabinet what I intended to do. The letter from the Secretary began politely enough but changed tone in the second paragraph:

> At the outset I should make it clear that you should rely on your own legal advice in considering the legal risks that may be associated with publication. Whether any legal action, criminal or civil, is initiated would be entirely a matter for the Commonwealth government and relevant authorities. The comments I make in this letter should not be taken as any indication, let alone commitment, that legal remedies may not be pursued.

He pointed out how, under the terms of section 70 of the *Crimes Act 1914*, I could be liable to imprisonment for up to two years. The letter then went on with an excellent presentation of the conservative case for the preservation of cabinet secrecy.

In passing, I would say that the thirty year rule applying to cabinet minutes and documents is an absurd rule at least in relation to domestic issues. Different considerations are involved in matters of foreign policy, security and intelligence. But for domestic matters the thirty year prohibition is simply a ban on knowledge and a severe handicap for serious scholars. Needless to say the fifty-year ban now placed on the cabinet notebooks, which record the cabinet discussions, is even more nonsensical. *A Cabinet Diary* records how this ban was put in place — it was a measure of the first Keating Government. A strong posse of cabinet ministers, backed by influential public servants, favoured burning the notebooks and they were only saved from the bonfire by a compromise that agreed to keep them from the public for fifty years.

Censorship, particularly of cabinet diaries, is the first constraint on keeping the two commandments. The second is length. Political diaries tend to be rather long documents. Those of Benn and Crossman run to several volumes. It is doubtful whether we have the market in Australia for such lengthy works. The tolerance of publishers again renders difficult the honouring of the two commandments.

Thirdly, editors of diaries become impatient with the state of the prose. Scribbling things down late at night or tiredly talking into a tape recorder do not produce limpid prose of the order of John Button's. So there is inevitably a problem of style suitable for publication. Fourthly, political diaries are more likely than other political writings to reduce a publisher's lawyers to apoplexy.

In the case of *A Cabinet Diary* how did we handle these constraints yet remain faithful to the two commandments?

On the wisdom of publication, given the letter from the Department of the Prime Minister and Cabinet, we relied on a generous interpretation of Lord Widgery's judgment in the Crossman case. It was Widgery's view, at least as regards domestic matters, that ten years and three elections was a sufficient time lapse to allow the publication of the Crossman diaries without any injury to the constitutional system. As thirty years had passed since the Widgery judgment and decisions had become more liberal we considered that six years and three elections were sufficient. I survived.

I did excise a few sensitive foreign policy and intelligence references, though there is a description of a Cabinet discussion of an intelligence fiasco. I do not think that these conventions should be used to shield the intelligence services from scrutiny of incompetence, provided, of course, that any revelations do not damage national security or endanger particular individuals.

On the length of the manuscript, the publishers required a reduction of 70,000 words from the original diary. How, then, do you remain true to the original diary? I resolved that there was a key theme dominating the diary and that was the first Keating Government's struggle to survive. Much material extraneous to that theme was cut. For example, a lot of constituency stuff was cut, a lot of parochial South Australian politics went, but all the material relating to the central theme was virtually untouched in substance.

Pruning the prose made it, hopefully, more lucid, but I tried to avoid any change in substance, tone or judgments. I did restructure the Cabinet discussions to make them easier for readers to follow but at the same time sought to remain true to the arguments advanced by the ministers. Finally, given the concerns of the libel lawyers, I modified a few intemperate remarks about senior colleagues and excised about a dozen candid comments on minor figures.

Writing Political Autobiographies

John Button

My own contribution to the 'John Button ego poll genre', as I call it, has always been unplanned and relates to circumstance. In my last two or three years in Parliament, after I had made it clear I had had enough of politics and wanted to leave, I had approaches, indeed pleadings, from seven publishers about writing my memoirs or autobiography. I did not want to do that. I wanted to finish what I was doing in Parliament and then think about all that at a later stage. I never contemplated writing an autobiographical book at all. What I did want to write was the book I, in fact, *did* write — *Flying the Kite* (1994), a different kind of book because the topic really interested me, about my experiences travelling as a politician and particularly as a minister.

I had many experiences travelling. I thought these things should be shared. For instance, I went to Reagan's America once. The first lunch I had there was with David Packard, the founder of Hewlett Packard. He was very deaf, and he took out his hearing aid and put it in the middle of the table. I did not know throughout the entire lunch whether I should speak at the hearing aid or at him. I had a terribly embarrassing time. The same with a quasi-criminal prime minister of Ireland called Charles Haughey. He was a delightful fellow but thoroughly wicked.

After *Flying the Kite* publishers would say to me, what about the memoirs? At that time I was writing a column for the *Sydney Morning Herald* and *The Age*. Some of these columns were published as a book called *On the Loose* in 1996 which has some of my best writing, if I might say so myself. *As it Happened* waited until 1998. By the time I got round to it I was really a bit exhausted.

How did I approach the writing of my memoirs? First, I did not do it very deliberately, not at all in fact. It came, in a sense, as a response to publishers. As I say in the book, I had no diaries — just occasional little notes to myself, some of which I did put in diaries — comments like: 'I decided today that the prime minister is clinically insane'. I put little notes like that in diaries on key occasions, but nothing else. So I started a bit behind with what I called the *bric-a-brac* of a political career — press clippings, scrawled notes and letters from friends and enemies. I checked on many facts with staff and party colleagues.

What I tried to do was hang the narrative around various events or experiences which were particularly vivid to me. Many of those events were outside politics. For example, I was involved with a theatre in Melbourne which was a wonderful experience — quite depressing and bizarre in some ways, but still wonderful.

I always had something of an ambivalent relationship with politics. I enjoyed it, but I also had other interests. Every night I read for an hour before I could go to sleep, unwinding, and I read novels. It was about unwinding from the day's politics. When we were ministers, Neal Blewett and I used to sneak off to the movies together. That was regarded as very abnormal behaviour in Parliament. There were very few people who read books in the Parliament, and few people who were interested in outside activities, certainly in Canberra.

Publishers of memoirs, of course, are concerned about commercial sales. I have to make the point that for ex-politicians who want to write, the progression from the first book to the third is downhill all the way. *Flying the Kite* sold 26,000 copies; by the time I got to *As it Happened* and *On the Loose* it was about 12,000 or 14,000 copies, so it went down very suddenly in four or five years.

What did I hope to do in *As it Happened*? I wanted to let people understand what politics was like and what it was like to be in politics. Above all, I wanted to make it readable, hoping more people would gain an understanding of a life in politics. I think now I was very unsuccessful in this because what the book really says is what it was like for *me* to be in politics, not what it would be like for the *reader* to be in politics. In some sense, a daily diary gives a better picture of what it is like to be in politics. It captures the mundane nature of it all. Also it records what political people have said on particular occasions and this retains an importance.

Hence, in Britain, Alan Clark's diaries (1993-2000) are pre-eminent as a great political diary, not only because of what he records, but because he constantly illustrates his own personalities and neuroticisms. So, one diary entry starts: 'Woke up this morning feeling awful. I think my lymph glands have stopped working'; or, 'I had the hots for the redhead at the local exchange'. His diaries are really extraordinary, but eminently readable. I do not know what they sold but they are so readable. People will form a quite eccentric but nonetheless interesting view of the sort of things that happened in political circles. Often he is unserious: 'I was talking to my loathsome namesake Kenneth Clarke this morning, and he was going on about inflation, and I said to him have you ever been to Argentina? 2,000% inflation and you can still get a bottle of wine and a woman'. He is so politically incorrect! Yet you get a great insight into the political processes.

In Australia, Paul Hasluck's 'memoirs', *The Chance of Politics* (1997), are similarly important. I do not think any research was done for him; rather they are very personal reflections on colleagues and circumstances — and a very readable book. I also think Neal Blewett's memoirs (Blewett 1999) have similar insights in so many ways.

I recently reviewed Harold Macmillan's diaries (2003). You see the difference between diaries and biography if you look at Macmillan. His diaries are so boring;

the military moustache concealed a stiff upper lip — and did it ever! Here is a man who is in national politics and his wife is the mistress of a fellow Conservative for 34 years I think, and Macmillan never mentions that guy in a 600 page diary except in an aside about 'Loud mouth Boothby', as he calls him, and that is the only reference in the whole book.

There is also the dominant role of his mother. She arranged what class he was to be in at Eton. When he went to Oxford and his tutor was Ronald Knox. She thought that Macmillan was being influenced by this papist tutor and had Ronald Knox dismissed from the staff at Oxford — this sort of thing goes on throughout his life. At his wedding, when he married the Duke of Devonshire's daughter, and all the royal family are the guests of the bride. His mother then arranges for the Macmillan list of famous authors to be the guests of the bridegroom. So Henry James and all sorts of people find themselves at this wedding. They had no idea they were there merely to balance up the royal family. In the diaries there is not a hint of that sort of thing.

So, what *should* we write on in political autobiography? It is a very subjective question. I think the answer is that you write about the things which have impinged on your consciousness and try and write them as well as possible and share them with the reader. The role of political memoirs only seems to me to be a very limited one. It gives a personal but more rounded picture to a period, or a government, and the way in which a government works.

If readers want to understand more systematically what happened in my political life, then read *Dodging Raindrops* (Weller 1999). First of all it is well researched. I had no researchers. I just plucked things out of the air and wrote about them. But Pat Weller had a fantastic researcher, sort of like a daschund after a truffle. She went everywhere and I learned a lot about my family which I never previously knew. She found out, for example, that one of my great-great-grandparents was a tobacconist in London and owned property in America, and three or four brothers were killed in the American civil war defending the family's tobacco properties. I knew nothing about all that.

Finally, I wish to underline one last distinction. There is a huge difference between professional biographers and amateurs. The professional biographer plans a work and researches it. The amateur does not. The amateur has to rely on flair, if possible, and the amateur generally gets larger indulgence from reviewers. Amateurs have to rely on titles like *Flying the Kite*, *On the Loose*, *As it Happened* — what they lack in self-discipline, they have to make up for in accessibility and charm.

Political Biographies and Administrative Memoirs: Some Concluding Comments

Philip A. Selth

When I was invited to write this conclusion, I was asked not to give potted summaries of the earlier contributions. Rather, my task was to consider some of the major themes and issues that stand out from the collection of contributions presented for this monograph. I will do this by framing key questions for political biographers.

What is 'political biography' — and does the description matter?

The Australian and New Zealand School of Government workshop on political biographies proceeded on the basis that 'political biography' was a genre in its own right. This was reinforced by the fact that most of those attending the workshop were political scientists — or, at least, have been political science students. Geoffrey Bolton said that 'real intellectuals do not do political biography', that political biography 'is doubly suspect because it carries with it a whiff of the "great man in history" heresy', and 'is also prone to contamination with a moral agenda, or at the very least to an implication that the lives of past statesmen may convey lessons and examples to the political leaders of our own generation'. Yet, as Bolton stated, and the workshop attested, 'political biography survives'.

In her introductory essay, 'Political Biography: its contribution to political science', Tracey Arklay claimed that 'political biography is the form through which writers breathe life into archival documents such as letters, diaries, birth, death and marriage certificates, Hansard and official records to assist in the re-creation of a life'. She noted the comment by Harold Lasswell, Professor of Law and Political Science at Yale, that 'political science without biography is a form of taxidermy' (quoted in Walter 1980) or as Sir John Seeley, the nineteenth century historian, put it: 'history without political science has no fruit; political science without history has no root'. As Michael Holroyd (2003: 30) has written: 'biography began as a reinforcement of the existing order. By re-examining the past and pointing it in a new direction, it may now be used to question our understanding of the present, and affect our vision of the future'. Judith Brett (1997: 1) put it succinctly in *Political Lives*: 'the task of political biography is to tell the story of a political life in such a way as to make that life intelligible'.

Why should we be concerned that 'political biographical methodology on the whole [is] so ill-defined'? A good biography can 'provide students of politics with another perspective of how power is shared, how leaders are made not born, and how circumstances can catapult ordinary people into extraordinary situations'. Few would disagree with any of these sentiments. But are we not talking about biography as such. Is there a sub-species of 'political biography'? Does it matter? What *is* 'political biography'? Robert Porter (1993: 1) tells us that political biographies in Australia 'have typically been written on those who have attained leadership of their political party or of government'. There are few memoirs and biographies of the backbencher (St John 1969; Haylen 1969; Hermann 1993; Fry 2002; Duthie 1984; Gullett 1992; Kane 1989; McManus 1977). This is not surprising. It would be an unusual publisher who is interested in a book about someone few book buyers had heard about. There is also the practical problem of the record to be examined. 'A great man leaves a trail behind him — press reports, letters, official records, and a wide circle of acquaintances who also have letters and the rest, in which he is mentioned' (Pimlott 1990: 223). The emphasis at the workshop was on biographies (and biographers) of the twentieth century, and mainly Australian federal politicians; that is, on leaders of government. There have been many references to Allan Martin's two-volume biography of *Menzies: A life* (1993; 1999) but few to his *Henry Parkes: A biography* (1980). Disregarding the 79 years between the subjects' birthdates, I suggest there is no difference in subject matter that would have the latter work labelled a 'political biography' and the former not.

If Ben Pimlott's *Harold Wilson* (1992) and *Hugh Dalton: A life* (1985) are political biographies, because they were prominent in national government, is Pimlott's *The Queen: A biography of Elizabeth II* (1996) a political biography? Are John Toland's *Adolf Hitler* (1976) and Richard Bosworth's *Mussolini* (2004) political biographies? Andrew Roberts recently published a dual biography of Napoleon and Wellington (2002). Is this a political biography? The issue is the interaction between personality and office, between government and private passions — even in people for whom governing was not their primary motivation or interest.

General Ulysses S. Grant's *The Personal Memoirs of U.S. Grant* (1895), one of the best written memoirs of which I am aware, is generally classified as being 'military memoirs', yet Grant was President of the United States for eight years. John Dean's biography of *Warren G. Harding* (2004) has recently been published in Arthur M. Schlesinger's series of books on American presidents, an interesting choice of author given Harding's reputation. There is Winston Churchill's very successful attempt to influence how he would be seen by both his contemporaries and history, *The Second World War* (1948-56). Few biographies bluntly state in their title that the book is a political biography, as did Jenny Hocking for *Lionel Murphy: A political biography* (1997). All of these biographies could be labelled as 'political biographies'.

Trying to define a political biography is a sterile debate.[1] The approach I would prefer is rather to ask which biographies, autobiographies and memoirs have influenced political institutions (including the public service) or, more commonly, which ones show how these institutions work. It is these works that have lasting value for political scientists. Jessie Street's autobiography, recently edited by Lenore Coltheart, shows how this unelected campaigner for human rights influenced both Australian and international bodies (2004). In contrast, in her recent autobiography *Chika*, Kerry Chikarovski, the former New South Wales minister and Leader of the Opposition, shows us little of the inner workings of government — or Opposition (2004).

What is a good political biography — and what gets published?

According to Ben Pimlott (1990: 214) 'many people with a deep interest in politics, including quite a few practitioners, look to biography for knowledge and insight. But what is on offer so frequently disappoints'. Perhaps the best example of a biography that assists us in the understanding of a political system is Robert Caro's magisterial *The Years of Lyndon Johnson* (Caro 1982; 1989; 2002). Three volumes down, and Johnson has still to campaign for the White House in 1960. Caro's brilliant work is not a mere biography, but more a series of superb accounts of political institutions influenced by, or having an influence on, LBJ. The first 105 pages of the most recent volume, *Master of the Senate*, is an account of the Senate seniority and committee system; how the Southern Senators stitched up the committee system and ran the Senate as their personal fiefdom. It could have been a volume on its own. As Caro notes on his webpage: 'to show power truly you not only have to show how it is used but also the effect on those whom it is used. You have to show the effect of power on the powerless.'

On the basis of an informal survey to establish our favourite Australian 'political biographies', Tracey Arklay pointed out that of the top five biographies (Watson 2002; La Nauze 1965; Day 1999; Brett 1992; Weller 1989), all were about a prime minister, although only two that have been selected are biographies in the traditional sense of the word. However, all of them tell us about how we are governed, explain the thinking of past leaders, and contribute to political science by illustrating how personalities affect our political structures and policy. Whatever the reason for the selection of these books — one thing is certain — all have contributed to a greater understanding of how politics works. That is probably reason enough.

There is very little point in writing a biography that no one will read. They need to be published — and to be published they need to sell. As Pimlott has noted, among book-buyers, 'celebrity is the draw, quality is secondary. It is, perhaps, this market pressure that is most responsible for making the generality of political biographies valets to the famous' (Pimlott 1990: 223). It is a great pity that a work of such value as Geoffrey Bolton's *Edmund Barton: The one man for the job* (2000) would not have been published by Allen & Unwin without the financial support of the National Council for the Centenary of Federation. Would John La Nauze's (1965) two-volume *Alfred Deakin: A biography*, far better as political history than it is as a biography, readily find a publisher today?

Perhaps not surprisingly, the majority of Australian political biographies and memoirs are of Labor figures. Is this because, as Pat Weller speculated, the Liberals appear to have no heroes other than Menzies? At the state level, Sir Henry Bolte, Sir Charles Court and Sir Thomas Playford might rate as heroes (Prior 1990; Blazey 1972; Crocker 1983; Cockburn 1991; Court 1995). Or is it, as Ian Hancock suggested, unlike Labor, the Liberals are not interested in the past? Is it because many Liberal politicians, when they leave parliament go into business to make money and do not have the time or inclination to pen their memoirs? This imbalance may well say something about the different approaches to life across the party divide, or something about Labor's capacity for myth-making and calamity. It is to be hoped that the gaps in our studies of Liberal and Country Party leaders at both federal and state level will soon be overcome.

What are the publishers looking for? Clearly, it is a book that will make a profit. Unfortunately, the market in Australia for a biography is small. There is not the opportunity for newspaper serialisations that in, for example, the United Kingdom, would bring in large sums for both the publisher and author. Here a political biography may get a page in the *Canberra Times*. But if the subject is a sporting hero, he or she may get several pages in the *Sydney Morning Herald* or more in the *Daily Telegraph*. Regrettably, the role of celebrities, gossip and hype are more likely to find a wider market than an in-depth, analytical biography of a political figure that eschews the subject's private life.

In April 2005 *The Australian* published a list of 'political autobiography sales' that makes interesting reading:

Bob Hawke	*The Hawke Memoirs* (hardback)	75,000
Graham Richardson	*Whatever It Takes*	45,000
Bill Hayden	*Bill Hayden: An autobiography*	42,383
Cheryl Kernot	*Speaking for Myself Again*	4,000
Neal Blewett	*A Cabinet Diary*	3,000
Kerry Chikarovski	*Chika*	295

Fortunately, despite the best efforts of the federal government in recent years, there is still funding for academics to conduct long term, in-depth research. The recent books by, for example, Judith Brett, David Day, Ian Hancock, Geoffrey Bolton and Pat Weller, to pick but a few, clearly benefited from the authors having institutional support, if only indirectly. We should also not forget the contribution that has been made to Australian scholarship by the thousands of entries in the *Australian Dictionary of Biography* , the editorial staff of which are housed in The Australian National University's Research School of Social Sciences. Many books and articles about Australian politics and government, and biographies, owe their origin to an entry in the *ADB*. A few owe their origin to a masters or doctoral thesis, usually extensively reworked before publication. There is also the valuable *The Biographical Dictionary of the Australian Senate* (Millar 2000; 2004).

John Iremonger, who died in 2002, published the works of many of our best political biographers. One of the last books Iremonger commissioned was Chris Masters' forthcoming biography of the radio personality Alan Jones. So far as I am aware, Mr Jones has never been elected to public office. Yet he very clearly meets the Australian Concise Oxford Dictionary definition of being a politician, 'a person engaged in or concerned with politics, especially as a practitioner'. It is possible that Alan Jones has more influence on New South Wales politics than anyone other than the Premier. If he raises an issue on his morning radio program critical of the government, efforts will be made to have that issue settled before lunchtime. Once Chris Masters' book has run the gauntlet of the defamation lawyers and is published, it will tell us as much about politics and government in New South Wales as the raft of books by and about New South Wales politicians that have been published in recent years (for example, Steketee and Cockburn 1986; Cumming 1991; Collins 2000; Dodkin 2003; West and Morris 2003).

Unfortunately, in Australia few diaries by politicians have been published and certainly nothing comparable to the Crossman (1975-77), Castle (1980) and Clark (1993) diaries. Only three by recent federal politicians come to mind, those by Howson (1984), Cameron (1990) and Blewett (1999). Blewett's is by far the most analytical and useful, especially for its musings on the way cabinet was run and how effective the procedures might be (Weller 2005). There is also the promise of Mark Latham's diaries, which are being published by Melbourne University Publishing in September 2005 (Latham 2005; Lagan 2005). At the state level, we know Bob Carr is keeping a diary, extracts of which are finding their way into books (Dodkin 2003).[2] But, as Neal Blewett has cautioned, care needs to be taken with diaries as much as with autobiographies and authorised biographies. Blewett edited his diaries for reasons of space. Presumably no diarist deliberately washes all his or her dirty linen in public. Those extracts from unpublished diaries that are made available to others are no doubt carefully selected by their author. Blewett also made the point that politicians' diaries are usually relentlessly political, dense, unselected and turgid. Diaries are rarely kept by the most senior ministers, probably because they do not have the time to do so (Carr appeared an exception to this rule).

Similarly, we need to exercise caution when drawing upon accounts by politicians who have a reputation to protect — and/or advance. The former Liberal politician, Peter Coleman, was recently reported as saying that political memoirs 'are usually full of lies and spin and quickly fill the remainder shelves'. Neal Blewett reminded us that Bob Hawke's massive memoir tells us little about the fall of Susan Ryan as a minister, Indonesia or the sinking of the dollar after its deregulation in December 1983. The account of how he became leader is benign. As Pat Weller noted, autobiographies are about highlights in the author's life, not routine. For John Button, personal accounts can be both informative and a pleasure to read. He tried in *As It Happened* (1998), very successfully, to show what it was like to be in politics, and to make the book readable. He hung his narrative around events that were of interest to him, not all of which were political.

The memoirs of prime ministers Whitlam (1985) and Hawke (1994) are clearly intended, at least in part, to influence the way in which their governments will be regarded in the future. Peter Walsh's *Confessions of a Failed Finance Minister* (1995) is both a defence of the economic and social policies Walsh espoused and a bitter attack on those policies and individuals he opposed. The recently published *In Command of History* (2004) by David Reynolds shows how the prime motivations for Churchill writing his *The Second World War* were to secure his reputation and to shape our understanding of the conflict and our image of Churchill the prime minister. Another was to make money. Churchill had no hesitation in distorting the truth and censoring the records to achieve his aim. But he achieved his purposes.

Questions of Sources and Methodology

The term 'triangulation' was used to describe what many regard as basic research — checking and double checking information. As Pat Weller put it, when there were two in the room, if you can, ask both what happened. Political scientists (and others) should stop using jargon. Simple English will suffice. Indeed, the term 'triangulation' is far better known to political scientists as being the term used by Clinton adviser Dick Morris to explain his policy of urging Clinton to distinguish himself from congressional Democrats as well as congressional Republicans (Morris 1999).

Ian Hancock noted the wealth of material available in the National Archives of Australia (NAA) on the Liberal Party that seem to have been mined by few. Lenore Coltheart referred to the value of the World Wide Web, and in particular the National Archives' website devoted to Australian prime ministers and to its 'uncommon lives' pages, in particular those for Jessie Street.[3] The Archives' collection on Australia's prime ministers including documents, photographs, sound, films and videotape, and the links to many other collections, is an essential reference source for anyone working on the life and times of the prime ministers.

The NAA website is a virtual nod in the direction of the American presidential libraries, which have spawned so many great (and not so great) biographies. Nicholas Brown spoke of what will be an outstanding contribution to the study and writing of Australian biography, the project to publish the *Australian Dictionary of Biography Online* in fully searchable form with links to other archival and bibliographical resources.

Neal Blewett wrote about the debate in Cabinet in July 1992 concerning the destruction or retention of the notebooks used by Cabinet Office staff who attend Cabinet meetings and prepare the minutes. The notebooks are now permanently retained, but unlike most Commonwealth records are not available until 50 years have elapsed.

On a personal note, when the *Archives Bill 1983* was being drafted, I together with George Nichols — the then First Assistant Secretary, were among the cabinet officers arguing that the notebooks should be brought within the provisions of the proposed legislation and permanently retained. Perhaps not coincidentally, we both had degrees in history. Our view did not prevail. That Bill did not refer to the cabinet notebooks. Their existence continued to be, if not a secret, not publicised. However, early in the 1990s the view strongly argued by several senior officials (in both the Department of the Prime Minister and Cabinet and the NAA, where Nichols was Director-General) that if the notebooks were not brought under the *Archives Act* there was a real risk that some day there would again be attempts to destroy these valuable records prevailed and their proposed retention went before Cabinet. The *Prime Minister and Cabinet (Miscellaneous Provisions) Act 1994* brought the notebooks under the control of the Archives with the 50 year release date. It was a near run thing.

But a word of caution to those slavering at the thought that one day they will be able to access the cabinet notebooks. I doubt that at least some of the entries in the notebooks (assuming they can be read) will tell us more than what is already known through the minutes. In my time in the Cabinet Office (1980s), there were no rules about how and what was to be recorded in the notebooks. Each note taker made such notes as he or she thought would be useful when writing the minutes.[4]

In *A Cabinet Diary* Neal Blewett tells how he had deliberately refrained from any consultation of the cabinet notebooks in writing his diary. He would have had access to the cabinet submissions and minutes at the time. There is a convention that former ministers may 'refresh their memory' of the cabinet records they saw when in office when writing their memoirs. That access used to be generously granted, although the letter Blewett read to the workshop, written to him by Max Moore-Wilton, at the time Secretary of the Department of the Prime Minister and Cabinet, suggests that access may in more recent years have been less readily available.

Before leaving the subject of cabinet records, I offer one further personal anecdote. When I was a cabinet officer, Peter Edwards had recently been appointed the Official Historian of Australia's involvement in Southeast Asian conflicts. He had been granted unrestricted access to cabinet and departmental records. One day, while Peter was sitting in the Cabinet Office tapping away at a manual typewriter, staff were cleaning out the large walk-in vault where the records were kept. They found on a back shelf an envelope that had been sealed by Sir John Bunting, Cabinet Secretary from 1959-75. That envelope contained the original correspondence between the Australian and other governments concerning our entry into the Vietnam War. There may have been no other copies of at least some of this correspondence, which was promptly copied and made available to Edwards. The originals were despatched to the Australian Archives.

Since the advent of the Freedom of Information legislation and e-mail, the biographer and historian of the future will find the written records of the public services very sparse in contrast to the records before, say, the 1970s. The ubiquitous detachable yellow post-it notes are a boon to the public servant concerned with a future FOI request, but a curse to the researcher.

Who owns the story, and how far should one delve into the private as distinct from public life?

Most Australian political biographies tend to concentrate on the office rather than the individual. Paul Strangio's well received *Keeper of the Faith: A biography of Jim Cairns* (2002) is an exception to this rule, giving as it does a balanced account of Cairns' personal integrity with his failure as a minister. While not a biography in the traditional sense, Judith Brett's, *Robert Menzies' Forgotten People,* is another instance where the influence of the private life on the public life is critically examined. Pat Weller has made clear that, in his books on Malcolm Fraser and John Button, he was concerned not with writing a biography but with the way political institutions work, the way power is exercised, the interactions between individuals and the institutions in which they work and which they in part shape and which shapes them. When the office door closed, he lost interest in their lives.

Yet as Geoffrey Bolton pointed out, reticence to look into the private life can detract from the value of a political biography. He cited as an example Ross McMullin's generally lively and informative study of Labor Prime Minister Chris Watson (2004) that tersely informs us that Watson's premature retirement from federal politics was due to his wife's complaints about his frequent absences from home in Sydney. 'One would never know that Watson's concern for his wife arose partly because his presence helped her in a battle against alcoholism, nor that after her death he re-married and somewhat belatedly found fulfilment as a parent'.

There is clearly a problem in writing about a living person. The restrictive defamation laws across Australia are an obvious hurdle. Jenny Hocking was not the first biographer to find that her subject, the lawyer, politician and judge, Lionel Murphy, 'lived a prodigious public life, and yet remained an intensely private man'. There is also the problem such as that faced by Tim Rowse, to whom Nugget Coombs and his family made clear that Coombs' private life was out of bounds. As Rowse notes in the Introduction to *Nugget Coombs: A reforming life* (2002), 'The resulting book is more impersonal than most readers of biographies would wish'. There is no such reluctance to inquire into a subject's personal life in, for example, David Day's *Chifley* (2002) where the prime minister's extramarital affairs are examined in detail and the reader is taken literally into Chifley's bedroom. Bob Hawke's biographer (and now wife), Blanche d'Alpuget, made no secret of her subject's drinking problem.

The question is, how far do you need to go to understand the person about whom you are writing? Some in the media prefer the view from the bedroom or the hotel bar. I simply question whether this is always a relevant view. On the other hand, it is at least arguable that a good biography does not make a distinction between the subject's public and private life. While the subject's life should be the focus of intensive study, it should also be the vehicle for a wider observation of human nature and the human condition. 'If it is relevant to a biographer of Churchill that he was a failure at Harrow, it is relevant to a biographer of Atlee that he had a difficult wife and to a biographer of Lloyd George that he kept a mistress' (Pimlott 1990: 222). Bolton noted Laurie Fitzhardinge's reluctance to refer to Billy Hughes' fear of homosexual rape and the influence this must have had on Hughes' attitude to the possession and use of power in a Hobbesian world of potential violence, and to La Nauze being temperamentally unsuited to the sympathetic explanation of Deakin's mystical streak.

Jim Walter argued that a good political biography, particularly one written about someone still living or recently dead, is not written for the political party, the leader and acolyte. While the author needs to be aware of these sensitivities, he or she should be writing for those whose lives were affected by their subject. In Walter's view, that is who you are trying to write for — not necessarily to give them what they want, but to persuade them of why things turned out as they did, why things happened in the way they happened. His anecdote about the reviewer who complained that *The Leader* 'didn't give my Whitlam back to me' well illustrates the problem an author faces when writing about a prominent figure who has inspired both hate and admiration.

Because the subject of the biography may have been dead for many years does not provide an author with immunity from criticism by members of the family and friends, as David Day found when *Menzies & Churchill at War* (1986), *John*

Curtin: A Life (2000) and *Chifley* (2002) were published. The shorter the period of a writing after the death, clearly the greater the angst that will arise when dealing with the family. As Virginia Woolf put it: 'The widow and the friend are hard task masters' (cited in Pimlott 1990: 219).

I recently wrote an entry for the *Australian Dictionary of Biography* on Harold Bayard Piper, chief judge of the Arbitration Court during the Second World War (vol 16, 6). I would like to expand that entry into a long article or book. For a range of reasons, I have yet to do so. I feel a little uncomfortable at my dilatoriness because Piper's family were very generous to me in making material available and extending hospitality when I visited Melbourne for research. Our views on Piper differ a little. This is a problem faced by those who write about the living or where there is a living family. Few take the robust view John Gorton did when, in essence, he told Ian Hancock that as his biographer he could write whatever he liked about him, and went out of his way to assist Hancock obtain access to those who knew where a skeleton might be buried. It is a great pity more biographical subjects do not adopt the Duke of Wellington's approach of 'publish and be damned!' when the courtesan Harriette Wilson threatened to publish her memoirs and his letters.

There is the difficulty of either liking or disliking your subject. Tracey Arklay referred to coming to like her subject, Arthur Fadden. I respect Piper. When David Marr wrote the biography of Garfield Barwick (1980) he started not liking his subject because of his role in the 1975 Dismissal, but otherwise knew almost nothing about him. However, as he came to know more about Barwick, Marr came to discover much to admire in the man, for example, his sheer skill of the advocate. Rae Wear (2002: xi) did not change her view that Joh Bjelke-Petersen's premiership was an authoritarian and undemocratic regime, but she was compelled to 'acknowledge and try to take account of alternative perceptions and his disarming qualities'. Fin Crisp knew and admired Ben Chifley (1960). As Geoffrey Bolton observed, Crisp presented Chifley 'as a sagacious and practical statesman, almost without fault whose vision Labor [then in Opposition in the federal parliament] needed to recover'.

The problem of gender bias

Biography has moved on since the writing of *Ecclesiasticus*: 'Let us now praise famous men and their fathers that begat them!' I am not sure that now there is such a bias, but rather the abysmal representation of women in parliament is the reason for there being so few biographies and autobiographies about Australian women politicians. Those that we have are, for the most part, of little value to the political scientist. (There is no shortage of major biographies of, say, Margaret Thatcher (Young 1989; Campbell 2000; 2003) and Indira Gandhi (Frank 2001).

In Australia there is Susan Ryan's *Catching the Waves* (1999). There is Cheryl Kernot's biography (O'Reilly 1998) and then autobiography (2002) (the reason for its low sales in part being because her book tour was cancelled immediately after Laurie Oakes' expose in *The Bulletin* and on *Channel 9* of her relationship with Gareth Evans). There are Dame Enid Lyons' several books of memoirs (c1949; 1965; 1972), and autobiographies by Zara Holt (1968) and Hazel Hawke (1992). There are Kerry Chikarovski's autobiography, *Chika* (2004), and Franca Arena's *Franca: My story* (2002). Pauline Hanson is covered in Margo Kingston's *Off the Rails: The Pauline Hanson trip* (1994) and John Pasquarelli's *The Pauline Hanson Story* (1998).

Other books include Junie Morosi's *Sex, Prejudice and Politics* (1975) and Anne Summers' account of her early life (2000); regrettably it appears that we are not going to see a volume covering her period as a senior adviser to the Prime Minister. After these, I am struggling to think of other books by and about women politicians, public servants and those who worked in and around a parliament house. One other book that should be noted, surprisingly not mentioned during the workshop, is Diane Langmore's *Prime Ministers' Wives: The public and private lives of ten Australian women* (1992). A woman whose account of her time in the federal Parliament House we sadly miss is that of Ainslie Gotto, although Ian Hancock has acknowledged his debt to her for the assistance she provided when writing *John Gorton: He did it his way* (2002).

Gaps in administrative memoirs

Regrettably, there is a dearth of administrators' memoirs, accounts by federal and state public officials of their working life. What we have is sparse and of uneven quality. Nor do we have books of the quality of Peter Hennessy's *Whitehall* (1989) and *Cabinet* (1986) that show in detail the inner workings of our public services. Pat Weller's forthcoming book on the federal cabinet may fill one gap, but where is the equivalent of *Whitehall*? Nor are there many good biographies of public servants.

One problem is the various secrecy provisions in public servants' employment conditions, and legislation that explicitly forbids the disclosure of information that has come to the public servant's notice in the course of their duties. They do not have the same opportunity, however limited, of Commonwealth ministers being able to 'refresh' their memory. There is also the strong tradition, although possibly now a bit frayed around the edges (Wilkie 2004) of public servants having a strong ethic of confidentiality. The various codes of conduct formally reinforce this traditional reticence. It is also probable that by the time most public servants have retired they do not feel inclined to spend their retirement researching their administrative past. Few serving (and former) public servants are prepared to speak on the record, although Pat Weller has left us a treasure trove in his *Australia's Mandarins: The frank and the fearless?* (2001) which draws upon interviews with over 100 past and present Commonwealth departmental heads. As Weller noted, 'If the public face of government can be found among the elected representatives, the public servants provide the sinews and muscle that make the body politic work' (2001: 3). No biography of a minister can ignore the influence he or she had upon their department — and that of the department on the minister.

There are, however, a few memoirs by senior federal (and state) public servants, although a number of agency histories now exist. There is a strong slant towards the memoirs of Foreign Affairs and Defence officers. There are a number of books and monographs about and by heads of the Department of Foreign Affairs, in particular.

Regrettably, we have very few accounts by career public servants which give attention to the administrative routine, rather than to career highlights. Richard Woolcott, the former Secretary of the Department and Foreign Affairs and Trade, makes clear in the title of his memoirs *The Hot Seat: Reflections on diplomacy from Stalin's death to the Bali bombings* (2003) where his primary interest lay. The occasional paper derived from the transcript of oral history interviews with one of his predecessors, Sir Keith Waller (1990), similarly favours diplomacy over administration. Sir John Bunting's affectionate memoir of a man he clearly admired, *R. G. Menzies: A portrait* (1988), tells a little about the relationship between one permanent head and his minister, but the emphasis is very much on Menzies rather than departmental administration. What we are told about the relationship of senior officials with the prime minister is very much the view of a mandarin and his regard for what he terms 'due process' (Bunting 1988; see also Hancock 2002). However, as Weller points out in his survey of research on the Commonwealth executive, Bunting's book is also 'an account, and a defence, of Cabinet government in the 1950s and 1960s' (2005: 36). John Menadue's account of his term as Secretary of the Department of the Prime Minister and Cabinet in *Things You Learn Along the Way* (1999) is a useful record of the development of that department's 'activist role' which started under Whitlam and continued under Fraser, and of the 'Loans Affair' and The Dismissal. He briefly covers his tenure as Ambassador to Japan and as Secretary to the Department of Immigration and Ethnic Affairs, and, later, Trade.

One exception, albeit slight, to the paucity of administrative memoirs by senior Commonwealth public servants is *They Also Serve* (1974), the memoirs of Sir William Dunk, chairman of the Commonwealth Public Service Board, 1947-1960. (Dunk preferred the term 'Notes' of his 'worm's eye view' through a full generation of official experience.) These notes include, for example, the detailed memorandum the Board put to Cabinet in June 1947 outlining 'the action the Public Service Board has taken, and the policies it proposes to follow, in carrying out its duties of staffing, organization and efficiency in the Public Service' at a time the service was being concentrated in Canberra. Dunk gives us an insight into his character when he tells us that Cabinet's acceptance of the Board's submission 'was a comfort (it is a useful thing to have a powerful piece of paper to wave under the nose of objectors)'. We also gain a slight understanding of his relationship with Prime Minister Menzies, who when asked on his appointment as prime minister in 1949, to endorse the memorandum 'gave a lordly wave of the hand and said "Carry on Sergeant-Major"'.

We also have Nugget Coombs' 'guarded and occasionally misleading account of his public life', *Trial Balance* (1981). Another account by a senior public servant, albeit in this instance one who did not look so favourably on his experience of the Australian public service, is that of Dr. V. G. Venturini. His vitriolic *Malpractice: The administration of the Murphy Trade Practices Act* (1980) covers his term as a commissioner on the Trade Practices Commission from early 1975 to 30 June 1977. Venturini does not share the affection for the public service which is so obvious in the works of Bunting and Dunk. To Venturini, the 'true bureaucracy — the *top* public service — still services: itself first and foremost, second, the rich; and moreover, it does that at the expense of the rest of the Australian community'. *No Grey Profession*, the memoirs of a director-general of the National Library, Harrison Bryan, are a far more sympathetic account of the institutions in which he worked, as are those of Frank Green, Clerk of the House of Representatives 1937-1955 (Bryan 1994; Green 1969).

While not a biography in the traditional sense, mention should be made of David Horner's valuable *Defence Supremo: Sir Frederick Shedden and the making of Australian defence policy* (2000). There is the biography of Robert Broinowski, secretary to three post-federation Ministers of Defence who retired in 1942 as Clerk of the Senate, written by his grandson, a former senior officer of the Department of Foreign Affairs and Trade (2001). But biographies of public servants are all too few. Peter Edwards' biography of Sir Arthur Tange adds to a very small library of major biographies of public servants, federal or state. While we have his memoirs, *Prosper the Commonwealth*, a biography of the first Secretary of the Commonwealth Attorney-General's Department, Sir Robert Garran, is long overdue. There are also the several books by and about Charles Perkins, the first departmental secretary of Aboriginal descent (Perkins 1975; Read 1990).

Conclusion

During the workshop reference was made to dozens of autobiographies, biographies and administrative memoirs that may help us to understand better how government and the public service work, why they work (if they do) in the way that they do, and how individuals, particularly senior politicians, both shape government and are, in turn, influenced by their political and administrative colleagues and processes. The quality of all these works is uneven;

it is a wonder some found a publisher. Others will be read, and mined, for years to come. The spread of publications across the federal and state arenas is also uneven, as it is across the various public sector agencies.

The term 'political biography' is of doubtful value, suggesting as it does some compartmentalised genre separate from the that of history or biography. Rather, what we are seeking are biographical accounts that contribute to our understanding of the Australian political and administrative systems. We are fortunate that we have many such works available to us. But many more are needed; from politicians, their staff, party officials, public servants and academics, journalists and others.

ENDNOTES

[1] It is bad enough that some historians still claim that biographers are mere showmen at best, quacks at worst. As Professor Patrick O'Brien, a former Director of the University of London's Institute of Historical Research put it, political biographies are informed by mere 'concerns to instruct and entertain their readers', and 'tell historians all too little about the core aspirations of their discipline, which are to acquire a proper understanding of evolving political institutions and processes' (!),cited in Pimlott 1990: 31).

[2] For Marilyn Dodkin's 2003 'Bob Carr: the Reluctant Leader', the author was granted access to Carr's private diaries.

[3] See http://uncommonlives.naa.gov.au/ also www.jessiestreetwomenslibrary.com).

[4] For an account of the purpose of the notes and their authority, see the Full Federal Court's decision in Commonwealth v Northern Land Council (1991) 103 ALR 267, esp. at 276-279 and the High Court's decision in Commonwealth v Northern Land Council (1993) 176 CLR 604.

References

Allen, Judith. 1994. *Rose Scott: Vision and revision in feminism*. Oxford University Press

Arena, Franca. 2002. *Franca: My story*. Simon and Schuster

Aubrey, John. 1965. *Brief Lives*. Oliver Lawson Dick (ed.) Penguin.

Barnett, David and Goward, Pru. 1997. *John Howard: Prime Minister*, Viking.

Beale, Howard. 1977. *This Inch of Time*. Melbourne University Press.

Bean, C.E.W. (ed). 1921-1942. *Official History of Australia in the War of 1914-1918*. 12 Volumes. Angus and Robertson.

Benn, Tony. 1987. *Out of the Wilderness: Diaries, 1963-67*. Hutchinson.

Benn, Tony. 1988. *Office Without Power: Diaries 1968-72*. Hutchinson.

Benn, Tony. 1989. *Against the Tide: Diaries 1973-76*. Hutchinson.

Benn, Tony. 1990. *Conflicts of Interest: Diaries 1977-1980*. Edited by Ruth Winstone. Hutchinson.

Benn, Tony. 1992. *The End of an Era: Diaries 1980-90*. Edited by Ruth Winstone. Hutchinson.

Bernstein, R. 1991. *The New Constellation*. Polity.

Bevir, Mark. 1999a. *The Logic of the History of Ideas*. Cambridge University Press.

Bevir Mark. 1999b. 'Sidney Webb: Utilitarianism, Positivism, and Social Democracy'. *Journal of Modern History*, 74(2), 217-252

Blazey, Peter. 1972. *Bolte: A political biography*. Jacaranda.

Blewett, Neal. 1999. *A Cabinet Diary*. Wakefield Press.

Blewett, Neal. 2002. 'No Secret Selves'. *Meanjin*, v.61, no.1, 2002: 4-19.

Blewett, Neal. 2004. 'The Post-Mortem'. *Australian Book Review*. Dec-2004-Jan 2005, 4-5.

Blondell, Jean. 1969. *An Introduction to Comparative Government*. Weidenfeld and Nicolson.

Blondell, Jean. 1981. *The Discipline of Politics*. Butterworth.

Bolton, Geoffrey. 2000. *Edmund Barton: The one man for the job*. Allen and Unwin.

Booker, Malcolm. 1980. *The Great Professional*. McGraw-Hill.

Bosworth, Richard J.B. 2004. *Mussolini*. Penninsular Publishing Company.

Bramson, Troy. 2003. 'Review of West and Morris, Bob Carr'. *Australian Quarterly*. Sept-Oct. 36-8.

Brett, Judith. 1992. *Robert Menzies' Forgotten People*. Macmillan Australia.

Brett, Judith. 1997. *Political Lives*, Allen and Unwin.

Brett, Judith. 2002. 'Review of Michael McKernan, Beryl Beaurepaire'. *Australian Journal of Politics and History*, vol 48 (2).

Brett, Judith. 2003. *Australian Liberals and the Moral Middle Class*. Cambridge University Press.

Britain, I . 2002. 'Life Writing — Editorial'. *Meanjin* Volume 61 (1) 2-3.

Broinowski, Richard Philip (2001). *A Witness to History: The life and times of Robert Arthur Broinowski*. Melbourne University Press.

Brown, Wendy. 1995. *States of Injury: Power and freedom in late modernity*. Princeton University Press.

Bryan, Harrison. 1994. *No Grey Profession*. Auslib Press.

Bryant, Sir Arthur. 1933–38. *Samuel Pepys* (3 volumes). Cambridge University Press.

Buckley, Ken et al. 1994. *Doc Evatt: Patriot, internationalist, fighter and scholar*. Longman.

Bunting, Sir John. 1988. *R. G. Menzies: A portrait*. Allen and Unwin.

Button, John. 1994. *Flying the Kite*. Random House Australia.

Button, John. 1996. *On the Loose*. Text Publishing.

Button, John. 1998. *As it Happened*. Text Publishing.

Cameron, Clyde. 1990. *The Cameron Diaries*. Allen and Unwin.

Campbell, John. 2000. *Margaret Thatcher: The grocer's daughter*. Jonathan Cape.

Campbell, John. 2003. *Margaret Thatcher: The Iron Lady*. Jonathan Cape.

Caro, Robert. 1982, 1989 and 2002. *The Years of Lyndon Johnson*. (v. 1. *Path to power*; v. 2. *Means of ascent*. v. 3. *Master of the Senate*). Alfred A. Knopf, Inc.

Carr, Bob. 2002. *Thoughtline: Reflections of a public man*. Viking/Penguin Books.

Carroll, John (chair). 2003. *Review of the National Museum of Australia, Its Exhibitions and Public Programs*. Department of the Communications, Information Technology and the Arts.

Castells, Manuel. 1988. *End of Millennium*. Oxford.

Castle, Barbara. 1980. *The Castle Diaries*. Weidenfeld and Nicolson.

Cavalier, Rodney. 2001. 'Review of David Day: John Curtin: a Life', *Australian Journal of Political Science*, 36(2), 2001, 382-4.

Chamberlayne, Prue; Bornat, Joanna; and Wengraf, Tom. 2000 (eds). *The Turn to Biographical Methods in Social Science: Comparative issues and examples.* Routledge.

Chapman, Richard A. 1988. *Ethics in the British Civil Service.* Routledge.

Chikarovski, Kerry, with Luis Garcia. 2004. *Chika.* Lothian Books.

Churchill, Randolph S. and Martin, Gilbert. 1966-1988. *Winston S. Churchill.* Eight volumes. Houghton Miffen.

Churchill, Winston, Sir (1948-56). *The Second World War.* Six Volumes (v.1. *The gathering storm*; v.2. *Their finest hour*; v.3. *The grand alliance*; v.4 *The hinge of fate*; v.5. *Closing the ring*; v.6. *Triumph and tragedy*). Cassell.

Claire Tomalin. 2002. *Samuel Pepys: The unequalled self.* Viking.

Clark, Alan. 1993-2002. *Diaries.* Three volumes (v1. *In power 1983-1992*; v2. *Into politics 1972-1982* (Ion Trewin, Ed.); v3. *The last diaries 1993-1999* (Ion Trewin (Editor)). Weidenfeld and Nicolson/Phoenix.

Clendinnen, Inga. 2004. 'In Search of the "Actual Man Underneath": AW Martin and the Art of Biography', *Conversations*, Volume 5, No 2, Summer 2005. 22-35

Cockburn, Stewart. 1991. *Playford: Benevolent despot.* Axiom.

Collins, Peter. 2000. *The Bear Pit: A life in politics.* Allen and Unwin.

Coombs, Nugget. 1981. *Trial Balance.* Macmillan.

Court, Charles, Sir. 1995. *Charles Court: The early years: An autobiography.* Edited by Geoffrey Blainey and Ronda Jamieson. Fremantle Arts Centre Press.

Crisp, L.F. 1961. *Ben Chifley: A political biography.* Longmans, Angus and Roberson.

Crisp, L.F. 1972. *Peter Richard Heydon, 1913-1971: A tribute from his friends.* L. F. Crisp.

Crocker, Walter. 1983. *Sir Thomas Playford: A portrait.* Melbourne University Press.

Crockett, Peter William. 1993. *Evatt: A life.* Oxford University Press.

Crossman, Richard H. S. 1975-77. *The Diaries of a Cabinet Minister.* Three volumes (v1. *Minister of Housing, 1964-66*; v2. *Lord President of the Council and Leader of the House of Commons, 1966-68*; v3. *Secretary of State for Social Services, 1968-70*). Cape.

Crowley, F. K. 2000. *Big John Forrest.* University of Western Australia Press.

Cumes, J.W.C. 1988. *A Bunch of Amateurs : The tragedy of government and administration in Australia.* Macmillan Company of Australia.

Cumming, Fia. 1991. *Mates: Five champions of the Labor right*. Allen and Unwin.

Cunneen, Christopher. 2000. *William John McKell: Boilermaker Premier, Governor-General*, UNSW Press.

d'Alpuget, Blanche. 1982. *Robert J. Hawke: A biography*. Schwarz/Lansdowne.

Damousi, Joy. 2001. *Freud in the Antipodes: A cultural history*. Menzies Centre for Australian Studies.

Davies, A. F. 1972. *The Task of Biography: Essay's in Political Sociology*. Cheshire.

Day, David. 1992. *Smugglers and Sailors*. AGPS Press.

Day, David. 1996. *Contraband and Controversy*. AGPS Press.

Day, David. 1999. *John Curtin: A life*. HarperCollins Publishers.

Day, David. 2001. *Menzies and Churchill at War*. Simon and Schuster.

Day, David. 2002. *Chifley*. HarperCollins Publishers.

Day, David. 2002a. *Whose Life is it Anyway?: The art of historical biography*. National Biography Award 2002 day of discussion 23.3.2002. (Session 3).

Day, David. 2002b. 'Cabinet Table and Kitchen Table'. *Meanjin*, Volume 61 (1) 2002: 35-39.

Deakin, Alfred. 1963. *The Federal Story: The inner history of the Federal cause, 1880-1900*. (First published 1944 by Robertson and Mullins). Edited and with an introduction by J.A. La Nauze. Melbourne University Press.

Deakin, Alfred. 1968. *Federated Australia: Selections from letters to the Morning Post 1900-1910*. Edited and with an introduction by J. A. La Nauze. Melbourne University Press.

Dean, John. 2004. *Warren G. Harding*. Times Books.

Dickens, A.G. 1959. *Thomas Cromwell and the English Reformation*. English Universities Press.

Dodkin, Marylin. 2003. *Bob Carr: The reluctant leader*. University of New South Wales Press.

Dunk, Sir William. 1974. *They Also Serve*. Public Service Board, Canberra.

Duthie, Gil. 1984. *I had 50,000 bosses: Memoirs of a Labor backbencher 1946-1975*. Angus and Robertson.

Edwards, John. 1996. *Keating: The inside story*. Penguin.

Edwards, P. G. 1997. *A Nation at War: Australian politics, society and diplomacy during the Vietnam War*. Allen and Unwin.

Edwards, P. G. with Pemberton, Gregory. 1992. *Crises and Commitments: The politics and diplomacy of Australia's involvement in Southeast Asian conflicts 1948-1965*. Allen and Unwin.

Ellis, Bob. 1997. *Goodbye Jerusalem*. Vintage.

Erikson, Erik H. 1959. *Young man Luther: A study in psychoanalysis and history*. Faber and Faber.

Evatt, H .V. 1938. *The Rum Rebellion*. Angus and Robertson.

Evatt , H .V. 1940. *Australian Labour Leader*. Angus and Robertson.

Fenno, R. F. 1990. *Watching Politicians: Essays on participant observation*. Institute of Governmental Studies, University of California.

Ferres, Kay. 2002. 'Gender, Biography and the Public Sphere'. In France and St Clair (eds), *Mapping Lives: The uses of biography*. Oxford University Press.

Fish, S. 1989. *Doing What Comes Naturally*. Oxford, Clarendon Press.

Fish, S. 1991. 'Biography and Intention'. In W. Epstein (ed). *Contesting the Subject: Essays in the post-modern theory and practice of biography and biographical criticism*. Purdue University Press.

Fitzgerald, Ross. 1994. *"Red Ted": The life of E. G. Theodore*. University of Queensland Press.

Fitzhardinge, L. F. 1964. *That Fiery Particle: A political biography of W. M. Hughes*. Vol 1. Angus and Robertson.

Fitzhardinge, L. F. 1979. *The Little Digger, 1914-1952: W. M. Hughes, a political biography*. Vol 2. Angus and Robertson.

Fitzherbert, Margaret. 2004. *Liberal Women: Federation to 1949*. Federation Press.

France, Peter and William St Clair (eds). 2002. *Mapping Lives: The uses of biography*. Oxford University Press.

Frank, Katherine. 2001. *Indira: The life of Indira Nehru Gandhi*. HarperCollins.

Fry, Ken. 2002. *A humble backbencher: The memoirs of Kenneth Lionel Fry: MHR Fraser, ACT 1974-84*. Ginninderra Press.

Gabay, A. 1992. *The Mystic Life of Alfred Deakin*. Cambridge University Press.

Garran, Sir Robert. 1958. *Prosper the Commonwealth*. Angus and Robertson.

Geertz, C. 1973. *The Interpretation of Cultures*. Basic Books.

Gergen, K. J. 1986. 'Correspondence versus Autonomy in the Language of Understanding Human Action'. In D. W. Fiske and R. A. Shweder (eds), *Metatheory in Social Science: Pluralisms and Subjectivities*. Chicago University Press.

Granatstein, J. L. 1982. *The Ottawa Men: The civil service mandarins, 1935-1957*. Oxford University Press.

Grant, Ulysses S. 1895. *The Personal Memoirs of U.S. Grant*. Sampson Low.

Green, Frank C. 1969. *Servant of the House*. Heinemann.

Gullett, H. B. (Henry Baynton). 1992. *Good Company: Henry "Jo" Gullett: Horseman, soldier, politician*. University of Queensland Press.

Hammersley, M. and P. Atkinson. 1983. *Ethnography: Principles in Practice*. Routledge.

Hancock, Ian. 2002. *John Gorton: He did it his way*. Hodder.

Hancock, Ian. 1996. 'Harold Edward Holt, 1908–1967'. *Australian Dictionary of Biography*, Vol 14, 474–80. Melbourne University Press.

Hancock, Ian. 2000. *National and Permanent?: The federal organisation of the Liberal Party of Australia 1944–1965*. Melbourne University Press.

Hancock, Ian. 2006. 'Robin William Askin'. In David Clune and Ken Turner (eds). *The Premiers of New South Wales — Volume Two 1901-2005*. Federation Press.

Harry, Ralph. 1983. *The Diplomat Who Laughed*. Hutchinson of Australia.

Hasluck, Paul. 1942. *Black Australians*. Melbourne University Press.

Hasluck, Paul. 1952 and 1970. *Government and the People*. 2 volumes: *1939-41* and *1942-45*. Australian War Memorial.

Hasluck, Paul. 1977. *Mucking About: An autobiography*. Melbourne University Press.

Hasluck, Paul. 1980. *Diplomatic Witness*. Melbourne University Press.

Hasluck, Paul. 1997 *The Chance of Politics*. Text Publishing.

Hawke, Bob. 1994. *The Hawke Memoirs*. Heinemann.

Hawke, Hazel. 1993. *My Own Life: An autobiography*. Text Publishing.

Hayden, Bill. 1996. *Hayden: An autobiography*. Angus and Robertson.

Haylen, Leslie. 1969. *Twenty Years' Hard Labor*. Macmillian of Australia.

Hazlitt, William. 1923. *The Spirit of the Age: Or, contemporary portraits*. Oxford University Press.

Henderson, P. G .F. 1986. *Privilege and Pleasure*. Methuen Haynes.

Hennessy, Peter. 1986. *Cabinet*. Basil Blackwell.

Hennessy, Peter. 1989. *Whitehall*. Secker and Warburg.

Hermann, Anton. 1993. *Alan Missen: Liberal pilgrim: A political biography*. Poplar Press.

Hocking, Jenny. 1997. *Lionel Murphy: A political biography*. Cambridge University Press.

Hofstadter, Richard. 1948. *The American Political Tradition and the Men Who Made It*. A. A. Knopf.

Holroyd, Michael. 2003. *Works on Paper: The craft of biography and autobiography*, Abacus.

Holt, Zara. 1968. *My Life and Harry: An autobiography*. The Herald.

Horne, Gerald. 2000. *Race Woman: The lives of Shirley Graham Du Bois*. New York University Press.

Horner, D.M. 2000. *Defence Supremo: Sir Frederick Shedden and the making of Australian defence policy*. Allen and Unwin.

Howson, Peter. 1984. *The Howson Diaries: The life of politics*. Viking Press.

Jenkins, Keith. 1995. *On 'What is History?'*. Routledge.

Jenkins, Roy. 2001. *Churchill: A biography*. Farrer, Straus and Giroux.

Johnson, Samuel. 'Biography', *The Rambler*, No. 60, Saturday 13 October 1750, in Donald Greene (ed.), *Samuel Johnson*, Oxford Authors, 1984, 204–217.

Kane, Jack (John Thomas). 1989. *Exploding the Myths: The political memoirs of Jack Kane*. Angus and Robertson.

Keating, Paul. 2000. *Engagement: Australia Faces the Asia-Pacific*. Macmillan.

Kernot, Cheryl. 2002. *Speaking for Myself Again: Four years with Labor and beyond*. HarperCollins.

King, Wayne. 1996. *Black Hours*. Angus and Robertson.

Kingston, Margo. 1999. *Off the Rails: the Pauline Hanson Trip*. Allen and Unwin.

Kirby, M. 2002. 'Notes on the Launch : Nugget Coombs: A Reforming Life', *Australian Journal of Public Administration*, 61(4): December 2002. 99-117.

Knight, R. 2005. 'Elusive fascination in Nelson's rite of passage'. *Panorama/Upfront*. Canberra Times. 2 July 2005. 8-9.

La Nauze, J. A. 1965. *Alfred Deakin: A biography*. Volume 1 an 2, Melbourne University Press.

Lagan, Bernard. 2005. *Loner: Inside a Labor tragedy*. Allen and Unwin.

Lake, Marilyn. 2002. *Faith: Faith Bandler, gentle activist*. Sydney.

Langmore, Diane. 1992. *Prime Ministers' Wives: The public and private lives of ten Australian women*. McPhee Gribble.

Lasswell, Harold. 1950. *Politics: Who gets what, when, how*. Peter Smith.

Latham, Mark. 2005. *The Latham Diaries*. Melbourne University Publishing.

Lawrence, Carmen. 2002. 'Talented artist sells his subject short' Evatt Foundation, 28.7.2002. (http://evatt.labor.net.au/news/70.html).

Lee, Janet. 2000. *Comrades and Partners: The shared lives of Grace Hutchins and Anna Rochester*. Lanham Md, Rowman and Littlefield.

Lieblich, A. Tuval-Mashiach, R. and Zilber, T. 1998. *Narrative Research: Reading, analysis and interpretation*. Sage Publications.

Little, Graham. 1988. *Strong Leadership: Thatcher, Reagan and an eminent person*. Oxford University Press.

Lyne, Charles. 1897. *Life of Sir Henry Parkes, Australian Statesman*. T. Fisher Unwin.

Lyons, Enid Muriel, Dame. c1949. *My Life: The illustrated autobiography of Dame Enid Lyons*. Colorgavure Publications.

Lyons, Enid Muriel, Dame. 1965. *So We Take Comfort*. Heinemann.

Lyons, Enid Muriel, Dame. 1977. *Among the Carrion Crows*. Rigby.

Macintyre, Stuart. 1991. *A Colonial Liberalism: The lost world of three Victorian visionaries*. Oxford University Press.

Macmillan, Harold. 1966. *Winds of Change, 1914-1939*. Macmillan.

Macmillan, Harold. 1967. *The Blast of War, 1939-1945*. Macmillan.

Macmillan, Harold. 1969. *Tides of Fortune: 1945-1955*. Macmillan.

Macmillan, Harold. 1971. *Riding the Storm, 1956-1959*. Macmillan.

Macmillan, Harold. 1972. *Pointing the Way, 1959-1961*. Macmillan.

Macmillan, Harold. 1973. *At the End of the Day, 1961-1963*. Macmillan.

Macmillan, Harold. 2003. *The Macmillan Diaries*: *The cabinet years, 1950-1957*. Peter Catteral (ed.) Macmillan.

Mann, Robert. 2002. 'Keating, the 'fanatic heart' PM. *The Age*. 13.5.2002.

Marr, David. 1980. *Barwick*, Allen and Unwin.

Martin, A.W. 1980. *Henry Parkes: A biography*. Melbourne University Press.

Martin, A.W. 1993. *Robert Menzies: A life 1894-1943*. Volume 1. Melbourne University Press.

Martin, A.W. 1999. *Robert Menzies: A life 1944-1965*. Volume 2. Melbourne University Press.

Matthews, Gordon. 1996. *An Australian Son*. William Heinemann Australia.

McGahan, Andrew. 2000. *Last Drinks*. Allen and Unwin.

McKernan, Michael. 1999. *Beryl Beaurepaire*. University of Queensland Press.

McManus, Frank. 1977. *The Tumult and the Shouting*. Rigby.

McMinn, W.G. 1989. *George Reid*. Melbourne University Press.

McMullin, Ross. 2004. *So Monstrous a Travesty*. Scribe Publications.

Menadue, John. 1999. *Things You Learn Along the Way*. David Lovell Publishing.

Menzies, Robert. 1967. *Afternoon Light: Some memories of men and events*. Cassell.

Mill, J. S. 1969 [1840]. 'Coleridge'. In J. M. Robson (ed), *Essays on Ethics, Religion and Society. Collected Works of John Stuart Mill*. Vol 10. University of Toronto Press.

Millar, Ann (ed.). 2000, 2004. *The Biographical Dictionary of the Australian Senate*. Volume 1: 1901-1929 — Volume 2: 1929-1962. Melbourne University Press.

Morgan, Sally. 1987. *My Place*. Fremantle Arts Centre Press, 1987.

Morosi, Junie. 1975. *Sex, Prejudice and Politics*. Widescope.

Morris, Dick. 1999. *Vote.com*. Renaissance Books.

Murdoch, Walter. 1923. *Alfred Deakin: A sketch*. Constable.

Murphy, John. 2004. 'Review of Strangio, Keeper of the Faith'. *Australian Historical Studies*, 124.

Nethercote, J. R. 2002. 'Review of Nugget Coombs: A Reforming Life'. *Australian Journal of Public Administration*, 61(4): 103–106, December.

Neuman, W. Lawrence. 1997. *Social Research Methods: Qualitative and quantitative approaches*, Third edition. Allyn and Bacon, Boston.

Neustadt, Richard. 1960. *Presidential Power: The politics of leadership*. Wiley.

O'Reilly, David. 1998. *Cheryl Kernot: The woman most likely*. Random House Australia.

Ollard, Richard. 1974. *Pepys: A biography*. Hodder and Stoughton.

Osbourne, Robin. *Latham's World: The new politics of the outsiders*. http://echonews.com/1039/book_reviews.html

Osmond, Warren. 1985. *Frederic Eggleston: An intellectual in Australian politics*. George Allen and Unwin.

Parkes, Henry. 1971. *Fifty Years in the Making of Australian History*. Books for Libraries Press.

Partington, G. 1996. *Hasluck Versus Coombs: White politics and Australia's aborigines*. Quakers Hill Press.

Pasquarelli, John. 1998. *The Pauline Hanson Story by the Man Who Knows*. New Holland.

Paterson, Wendy. 2005. 'Australian Women's Political Activism: Early Influences'. *Australian Feminist Studies*. 20(46).

Patience, Allan. 2001. 'Review of Hocking, Lionel Murphy'. *Australian Journal of Political Science*. 36 (2), 595.

Pemberton, G. (ed). 2002. *Vietnam Remembered*. New Holland.

Perry, Harry C. 1923. *Memoirs of the Hon. Sir Robert Philp, K.C.M.G., 1851-1922*. Watson, Ferguson.

Perkins, Charles. 1975. *A Bastard Like Me*. Ure Smith.

Pimlott, Ben. 1985. *Hugh Dalton: A life*. Papermac/Jonathan Cape.

Pimlott, Ben. 1990. 'The Future of Political Biography'. *The Political Quarterly* 61 (2), 214-224.

Pimlott, Ben. 1992. *Harold Wilson*. HarperCollins.

Pimlott, Ben. 1994. *Frustrate Their Knavish Tricks: Writings on biography, history, and politics*. HarperCollins.

Pimlott, Ben. 1996. *The Queen. A biography of Elizabeth II*. HarperCollins.

Pimlott, Ben. 1999. 'Is Contemporary Biography History?' *Political Quarterly* 70 (1), 31-41.

Pimlott, Ben. 2002. *The Queen: Elizabeth II and the monarchy*. HarperCollins.

Plutarch (Mestrius Plutarchus). 1957. *Lives*. Edited by John Dryden (1631-1700) revised with an introduction by Arthur Hugh Clough. Dent.

Porter, Robert. 1993. *Paul Hasluck: A political biography*. University of Western Australia Press.

Prior, Tom. 1990. *Bolte by Bolte*. Craftsman Publishing.

Pusey, Michael. 2003. *The Experience of Middle Australia*. Cambridge University Press.

Radi, Heather. 1988. *200 Australian Women*. Women's Redress Press.

Read, Peter. 1990. *Charles Perkins: A biography*. Viking.

Renouf, Alan. 1980. *The Champagne Trail: Experiences of a diplomat*. Sun Books.

Reynolds, David. 2004. *In Command of History: Churchill fighting and writing the Second World War*. Allen Lane.

Reynolds, H. 2003. *North of Capricorn: The untold story of the North*. Allen and Unwin. 189-90.

Richardson, Graham. 1994. *Whatever It Takes*. Bantam Books.

Rickard, J. 1987. *H.B. Higgins: The rebel as judge*. Allen and Unwin.

Rickard, John. 1996. *A Family Romance: The Deakins at home*. Melbourne University Press.

Riggs, F. W. 1962. 'Trends in the Comparative Study of Public Administration'. *International Review of Administrative Science*. Vol. 28, 9-15

Roberts, Andrew. 2002. *Napoleon and Wellington*. Phoenix Press.

Rose. R. 2000. 'When and Why Does a Prime Minister Change?' *Transforming British Government Volume 2: Changing roles and relationships*, Rhodes, RAW (ed). MacMillan.

Rosenau, P. M. 1992. *Postmodernism and the Social Sciences: Insights, inroads, and intrusions*. Princeton University Press.

Ross, Lloyd. 1977. *John Curtin: A biography*. Macmillan.

Rowse, Tim. 2000. *Obliged to be Difficult*. Cambridge University Press.

Rowse. Tim. 2002. *Nugget Coombs: A reforming life*. Cambridge University Press.

Rowse, Tim. 2002a. 'Kinship of Failure'. *Meanjin*. 61 (1), 2002. 169.

Ryan, Susan. 1999. *Catching the Waves: Life in and out of politics*. HarperCollins.

Sanjek, R. (ed). 1990. *Fieldnotes: The making of anthropology*. Cornell University Press.

Seebohm, Caroline. 1997. *No Regrets: The life of Marietta Tree*. Simon and Schuster.

Sekuless, Peter. 1978. *Jessie Street: A rewarding but unrewarded life*. University of Queensland Press.

Seldon, Antony. 2004. *Blair*. Free Press.

Selth, P. 2002. 'Harold Bayard Piper' in J. Ritchie and D. Langmore (eds), *Australian Dictionary of Biography*, Volume 16. 6. Melbourne University Press.

Sennett, Richard. 1977. *The Fall of Public Man*. Knopf.

Seutonius, G. 1957. *Twelve Caesars*. (Translated by Robert Graves). Penguin.

Sexton, Michael. 1979. *Illusions of Power*. Allen and Unwin.

Sexton, Michael. 1981. *War for the Asking*. Penguin.

Simons, Margaret. 2004. *Latham's World*. Black Inc.

Skidelsky, Robert. 1975. *Oswald Mosley*. Macmillan.

Skidelsky, Robert. 1983-2000. *John Maynard Keynes: A biography*. Three volumes: v1. *Hopes betrayed, 1883-1920*; v2. *The economist as saviour*; v3. *Fighting for Britain, 1937-1946*. Macmillan.

Skidelsky, Robert. 2003. *John Maynard Keynes 1883-1946: Economist, philosopher, statesman.* (abridged edition). Macmillan.

Spender, Percy. 1969. *Exercises in Diplomacy.* Sydney University Press.

Spender, Percy.1972. *Politics and a Man.* Collins.

Spina, S. and Dodge J. 2005. 'It's about time: Catching Method up to Meaning — the usefulness of narrative inquiry in public administration research'. *Public Administration Review*, March/April 2005, Volume 65, No 2. 145-57.

St John, Edward. 1969. *A Time to Speak.* Sun Books.

Steketee, Mike and Cockburn, Milton. 1986. *Wran: An unauthorised biography.* Allen and Unwin.

Stirling, Alfred Thorpe. 1973. *On the Fringe of Diplomacy.* Hawthorn Press.

Strachey, Lytton. 1948. *Eminent Victorians.* Penguin/Chatto and Windus.

Strangio, Paul. 2002. *Keeper of the Faith: A biography of Jim Cairns.* Melbourne University Press.

Street, Jesse. 1966. *Truth or Repose.* Australasian Book Society.

Street, Jessie. 2004. *Jessie Street: A revised autobiography.* (Edited by L. Coltheart). Federation Press.

Sugden, E.H. and Eggleston, F.W. 1931. *George Swinburne: A biography.* Angus and Robertson.

Summers, Anne. 2000. *Ducks on the Pond: An autobiography 1945-1976.* Penguin.

Switzer, T. 2004. 'John Howard and the missing biographies'. *Quadrant.* 48: 38–40, October 2004.

Tange, Arthur, Sir. 1996. 'Plans for the world economy: hopes and reality in wartime Canberra. A personal memoir'. *Australian Journal of International Affairs*, v.50 no.3 Nov 1996. 259-267.

Tanner, J.R. 1925. *Mr Pepys.* G. Bell and Sons.

Theakston, Kevin. 1997. *Comparative Biography and Leadership in Whitehall.* Public Administration 75 (4): 651-667 Winter 1997.

Theakston, Kevin. 2000. 'Permanent Secretaries: Comparative Biography and Leadership in Whitehall'. In R.A.W. Rhodes (ed.), *Transforming British Government Volume 2: Changing roles and relationships*, Macmillan.

Tickner, Robert. 2001. *Taking a Stand.* Allen and Unwin.

Toland, John. 1976. *Adolf Hitler.* Doubleday.

Tomalin, Claire. 2002. *Samuel Pepys: The unequalled self.* Viking.

Tridgell, Susan. 2004. *Understanding Our Selves: The dangerous art of biography*. Peter Lang.

Trollope, Anthony. 1950. *An Autobiography*. Oxford University Press.

Trollope, Anthony. 2004 [1858]. *The Three Clerks*. With an introduction by W. Teignmouth Shore. eBooks@Adelaide. Available at: http://etext.library.adelaide.edu.au/t/trollope/anthony/clerks/.

Venturini, V. G. 1980. *Malpractice: The administration of the Murphy Trade Practices Act: antitrust as an Australian poshlost*. Non Mollare.

Waller, Sir Keith. 1990. *A Diplomatic Life: Some memories*. Centre for the Study of Australia-Asia Relations, Griffith University.

Walsh, Peter. 1995. *Confessions of a Failed Finance Minister*. Random House Australia.

Walter, James. (forthcoming). *Oxford Companion to Australian Politics*, Brian Galligan and R.W. Roberts (eds), Oxford University Press.

Walter, James. 1980. *The Leader: A political biography of Gough Whitlam*. University of Queensland Press.

Walter, James. 1986. *Ministers' Minders*. Oxford University Press.

Walter, James. 1998. 'Citizen Biographer'. In Tom Stannage, Kay Saunders and Richard Nile (eds), *Paul Hasluck and Australian History*. University of Queensland Press.

Walter, James. 2002. 'The Solace of Doubt? Biographical Methodology after the Short Twentieth Century'. In Peter France and William St Clair (eds), *Mapping Lives: The uses of biography*, Oxford University Press. 325.

Walter, James. 2005. 'Gough Whitlam: Bursting limitations'. In Judith Brett (ed), *Political Lives*, Allen and Unwin.

Warren, Robert Penn. 1946. *All the King's Men*. Harcourt Brace.

Watson, Don. 2002. *Recollections of a Bleeding Heart: A portrait of Paul Keating*. Knopf.

Watt, Alan, Sir. 1972. *Australian Diplomat: Memoirs of Sir Alan Watt*. Angus and Robertson in Association with the Australian Institute of International Affairs.

Wear, Rae. 2002. *Johannes Bjelke-Petersen: The Lord's Premier*. University of Queensland Press.

Weller, Patrick. 1985. *First Among Equals: Prime Ministers in Westminster systems*. George Allen and Unwin.

Weller, Patrick. 1989. *Malcolm Fraser PM: A study in Prime Ministerial power in Australia*. Penguin Books.

Weller, Patrick. 1999. *Dodging Raindrops — John Button: A Labor life*. Allen and Unwin.

Weller, Patrick. 2001. *Australia's Mandarins: The frank and the fearless?* Allen and Unwin.

Weller, Patrick. 2005. 'Investigating Power at the Centre of Government'. *Australian Journal of Public Administration,* Volume 64, Number 1, 2005. 35-42.

Weller, Patrick and Michelle Grattan. 1981. *Can Ministers Cope? Australian Federal Ministers at Work*. Hutchinson of Australia.

West, Andrew and Morris, Rachel. 2003. *Bob Carr: a self-made man*. Harper-Collins.

Wheatley, N. 2002 *'Whose Life Is It Anyway? The art of historical biography'* National Biography Award 2002 day of discussion 23.3.2002. (Session 3).

White, Hayden. 1973. *Metahistory*. Johns Hopkins University Press.

White, Hayden. 1978. *Tropics of Discourse*. Johns Hopkins University Press.

White, Hayden. 1987. *The Content of the Form*. Johns Hopkins University Press.

Whitlam, Gough. 1985. *The Whitlam Government 1972-1975*. Penguin.

Wilkie, Andrew. 2004. *Axis of Deceit*. Black Inc.

Woolcott, Richard. 2003. *The Hot Seat: Reflections on diplomacy from Stalin's death to the Bali bombings*. HarperCollins.

Wright, Maurice. 1969. *Treasury Control of the Civil Service, 1854-1874*. Clarendon Press.

Young, Hugo. 1998. *This Blessed plot : Britain and Europe from Churchill to Blair*. Macmillan.

Young, Hugo. 1989. *The Iron Lady: A biography of Margaret Thatcher*. Farrar Strauss Giroux.

Young, Hugo. 1990. *One of Us: A biography of Margaret Thatcher*. Pan Macmillan.

Index

www.ingramcontent.com/pod-product-compliance
Lightning Source LLC
Chambersburg PA
CBHW061240270326
41927CB00035B/3461